SHADOWS OF YESTERDAY

by Lisa L Colsen

The contents of this work, including, but not limited to, the accuracy of events, people, and places depicted; opinions expressed; permission to use previously published materials included; and any advice given or actions advocated are solely the responsibility of the author, who assumes all liability for said work and indemnifies the publisher against any claims stemming from publication of the work.

All Rights Reserved
Copyright © 2023 by Lisa L Colsen

No part of this book may be reproduced or transmitted, downloaded, distributed, reverse engineered, or stored in or introduced into any information storage and retrieval system, in any form or by any means, including photocopying and recording, whether electronic or mechanical, now known or hereinafter invented without permission in writing from the publisher.

Dorrance Publishing Co
585 Alpha Drive
Suite 103
Pittsburgh, PA 15238
Visit our website at *www.dorrancebookstore.com*

ISBN: 979-8-88729-137-6
eISBN: 979-8-88729-637-1

SHADOWS OF YESTERDAY

This book is dedicated to:

Retired Chief of Police, George McKay, for being such a very good friend to our family, during the long process of finding our sister. This book is also dedicated to my brothers and sisters, but most of all to Mom and my daughter who both struggled through the murders of their children. To my sister Sandi and my granddaughter, Avryonna.

We miss you all,

Dad
Mom
Calvin
Sandi
Oscar and Avryonna.

Love

Scientists know only what love does.

Love, properly applied, could virtually empty our asylums, our hospitals.

Love is the touchstone of psychiatric treatment.

Love can be fostered, extended, used to subjugate hate, and thus cure diseases.

More and more clearly every day, out of biology, anthropology, sociology, history, economics, psychology, the plain common sense, the necessary mandate of survival—that we love our neighbors as ourselves—is being confirmed and reaffirmed. Christ gave us only one commandment—Love…
Anon

Chapter 1

COLOSSIANS 3:13

Be gentle and ready to forgive, never hold grudges. Remember, the Lord forgave you, as you must forgive others.

LET ME INTRODUCE MYSELF. I AM LISA. I HAVE BEEN WRITING this book for more than forty-five years. I seem to never stop learning life, but do we ever? Or have life teach me. I hope to leave you with laughter, maybe some tears, a bit of joy and hope. The ability to smile after it all. To say, "Yes, God is good! I am blessed, and God surely loves me!"

So begins my story, but, also their story. I have pondered on the shocking, almost impossible events that occurred in my forty-five years of life. It will take me back to pain that I truly felt would drop me to my knees and did on occasions. To walk out of that dark place and be able to say I am a survivor!

In the year 1960, I was born to Calvin and Zelda Karnes, on the thirtieth of May. Born in the front seat of my dad's car. So began my life. The eighth child of a working, blue-collar, low-income family. On second thought, no, we were dirt poor.

This is not a book so much about my life, as about events that taught and left a few scars on me, how they affected me, in later years. How some I have worked through and some I still work on some forty-five years later. Because some scars don't come with a memory of—this is the day I got hurt. Others you search but never find the cut. Trying to still figure out what the results were supposed to be, and understanding some I may never figure out.

Memories of my childhood seem so dim and far away. Stuck in the dark recesses of my mind. Where memory seems so reluctant to go. Perhaps our minds protect us from bad experiences we have had. To accept our lives and go on to the next stage of our lives. And others stick in my mind as glue, to knock upon the windowpane of my soul, to which I do not want to answer. "Please leave, I am no longer home."

I was a sister to three brothers. Calvin (Cal), Oscar, and the baby of our family, Lonnie. There were six of us girls: Jean, Peggy, Connie, Kathy, Sandy (she spelled it Sandi) and me, the youngest of the girls. Most all my siblings were named after a relative, except for me. Mom always said her roommate in the hospital had a baby girl and that was her name. Mom liked it, so I became. I know earlier I said I was born in the car, but I still had to make my appearance there.

We were a large family; we were very poor. Did I know we were poor? Never. I followed my footsteps back through the path of my mind to a farm called the "Eighty," (simply called the 80, because it sat on 80 acres of land), which we lived on. It belongs to my grandpa and Grandpa Karnes. We lived there with Mom and Dad. I think life was very stressful for them both. My mom was fifteen when she got pregnant with my oldest sister. Back in the day, it wasn't socially acceptable to have children out of wedlock. Mom and Dad both worked to keep our large family fed. Mom had her ninth child at the age of thirty-two. I can hear the echo of my sisters, Stepmother Stella! Stepmother Stella, to my older sister who watched us all the time, while Mom and Dad worked.

When I was four years old, my brother Oscar, eight, my sister Sandi, six, and me sneaked away from our sister's sight. My dad was asleep on the couch. He had been working nights. We sneaked some matches and a little piece of an old dirty rag. We slowly helped each other up into the hayloft. We were on an adventure! We sat together in our little circle, in the middle of all that dry hay. We just wanted to see if we could get a little hay lit. We had the rag; we were going to put it out right away. As soon as we lit the match, it ignited, like it was gasoline! We tried putting it out but the little rag went up in flames along with all the dry hay. We all jumped out of the hayloft and ran to the house. The fire department was called, but, the barn was lost. I remember standing in the backend of Dad's pickup truck, watching the barn burn down and knowing we had done something terribly wrong. It would be something I would never be able to forget. My dad knew it was us, but he never said a word about the incident. I learned a valuable lesson that day. Just how fast a barn full of hay would burn, and life is precious. We were lucky to escape with our little lives.

My mom as a 14-year-old in Wisconsin.

My mom and dad abused alcohol. Soon after the fire, we moved. My dad either had to go to jail or go to treatment, so he chose treatment. Soon after he left, we moved and were put in foster homes. Me and Sandi were together in our foster home. Sandi was eight years old and I was seven. We stayed with Mr. and Mrs. Taroe. They made sure we were clean, that our hair was brushed, that we were bathed. But they were never our mom. Mr. Taroe, one night at the supper table told us we were going to get a spanking after supper for jumping on his van. I did not remember doing that but needless to say, it didn't make you want to hurry up and eat!

Sandi and I went out to the garage and he took my arm and had a rubber-handled hammer and spanked us with that. He let me go crying, and said, "Get in the house!" I lost my shoe and he picked it up threw it at me and hit me in the back of the head with it. Sandi babied me, but I just wanted my mom! We stayed in that foster home for one year. They fixed my crooked eyes. We reunited. Mom had gotten a farm place for us all. She rented from the man she worked for. Dad was no longer with us. He would come try to reenter our family, but Mom would not have it. My oldest brother always seemed to be the go-between with them two. I think it made his heart hurt.

Dad came with a gift one more time—a TV, which we never had. One more time going to my brother to ask Mom if he could come back and once again the answer was no. He then poured lighter fluid all over his clothes and struck a match and ignited himself. All I could think was how fast the dry yellow hay had burned. I remember his tears and how he smelled of burnt rag. He left that night and I was not to see him again for ten years. I believe with all the turmoil, we kids, at least us younger ones, were happy at this new farm. I can see in the distance the old barn with all the wild baby kitties and us chasing them, ducking under rusty barn pipes hoping to get ahold of one.

Can you hear the excited laughter! Finally getting a wild black baby lifting it to give it a hug to love her and tell her in a little girl voice, "Don't worry I will care for you." And having it reach my face and draw his teeth into my face! I was shocked! How could you do that? I just wanted to love you! She unlatched herself and she was gone. Lonnie went running in and told Mom right away. Back in those days iodine seemed to be the cure-all. So I got doctored by good old mecuricome. Which hurt worse than the bite itself!

My mother and dad

Chapter 2

EPHESIANS 6:2

Honor your mother and father. This is the first of God's Ten Commandments, that ends with a promise.

MY MOM TRIED SUPPORTING ALL NINE OF US KIDS WITHOUT THE help of a father in the home. I am sure it was very hard on Mom to have to take care of us all. To try to clothe us and keep food on the table. When I think back as an adult, I could never see how she could do all of this on her own. We soon moved to a house in town. Mom started staying out late or not even coming home. We kids took care of ourselves as best as little people knew how.

We lived in a two-bedroom apartment. The boys had one bedroom and the six of us girls shared the other. We had three beds in that one bedroom. Mom would sleep on the couch when she was home. We ran all over town. In the night and during the day. No one to oversee us. Mom, did love us I know. But at that time, I don't believe she really knew how to be a good parent to us. I believe everything was overwhelming for her without the help of our dad. I believe her own unaddressed abuse as a child left her in great emotional pain and alcohol and men, she thought, helped her feel accepted and loved.

When I was about seven years old, I drank my first drink. The world swirled and swirled I was actually drunk! I climbed the river bridge and was going to jump off, not because I wanted to die. But I thought I could fly! My brother who was five was with me and pulled me down and helped me back home. I wonder where now mom was at. And would I have drowned that day so long ago. If it were not for my brother. We were like wild creatures, that roamed the streets at night. Just like the stray cats that were in our barn years before. As soon as headlights would appear we scattered back into the darkness.

One night I awoke to my mom and sister fighting. My sister was about seven months pregnant. I climbed out of bed and they were standing on the stairs leading up to the apartments upstairs. my mom had been drinking and she was yelling at my sister words I didn't understand and pulling her hair and telling her she had to get out. My sister was crying and she left and soon after, I heard Mom's car start and roar off. I went back to bed beside my sister Sandi. She was a year older than me. She was my best friend. I felt safe with her. Soon I was awoken to my brother talking to my sisters saying he was leaving to go get Mom cause she had crashed her car into a tree. He had to go and get her before the police came.

I lay there waiting for Cal to bring our mom back home, in total fear for her. I lay in the dark, pretending I was asleep when she came into the bedroom. She lay there in the bed across from me. I watched her in the darkness. As she lit a cigarette and the strike of the match showed her face and the red ember grew brighter with each drag she took of the cigarette. And feeling so afraid for her. I knew she should not smoke in bed! Telling her in my secret thoughts. How very much I loved her. That no matter what she did I would always, always be there for her and love her no matter what!

The same year I first drank was the same year I smoked my first cigarette. I used to steal them out of my mom's pack she kept in her purse. Going out to the old outhouse the sun's rays streaking across my face through the cracks in the walls. The dust particles floating and crashing with the inhaled smoke 1 blew out of my little lungs, to crash and mingle together. Feeling my little head swim in dizziness. Knowing the feeling was nice. It's a form of your very first high. As when you are small and someone twirls you around and around and sets you down and you can't walk straight, but yet you are begging them to do it again because you liked the feeling it gave you.

my mother and her mother with my oldest sister and brother.

Chapter 3

HEBREWS 3:9

But God was patient with them forty years, though they tried his patience sorely; he kept right on doing his mighty miracles for them to see.

I THINK BACK TO THE SEVENTEEN YEARS MOM AND US KIDS LIVED with Ray. She was really not there a lot after the first five years. Our house sat in the same yard as my stepdad's bachelor brothers. One day a salesman came to the door. He asked if my mom was home. I said she was probably over at my stepdad's brother's house. I said I would run over there and get her. I ran as fast as I could, grabbed the railing, and swung myself onto the steps. Pulled open the screen door. There was my mom and my stepdad's brother in each other's arms, kissing! They jumped and moved apart. I felt like I had done something wrong.

I kept my eyes down and just said, "Mom, someone is here to see you." And ran never wanting to see or face either one of them. I was ten years old, but I knew in my heart, it was all wrong. When Mom returned to the house, she never mentioned what I had seen, or who knows maybe thought that they had parted before I had seen. I couldn't believe my mom would do that. I was sad! How could Ray's own brother betray his brother, and destroy our family!

Alcohol was once again reeling it's ugly head at us. It had always been a part of my life. I knew nothing else. Ray at the time him and Mom met and married was a recovering alcoholic. Soon Mom and my stepdad were drinking more than just Saturday night supper club nights. They were drinking at home. In the early part of 1975, me and Sandi decided we were going to California to see the ocean! Our adult supervision was basically nonexistent. I wasn't that keen on going at least not to see the ocean. But Sandi was the one who wanted to see it. To feel it's salty breeze across her face. I wanted to live her dreams with her.

One day when school got out for the summer. We packed a suitcase and left my sister's house. We ditched the suitcase just out of town. It was too heavy to carry. We didn't even take an extra change of clothes! We hitched a ride to the freeway. On the freeway we got a ride from a man who was running a carnival and he asked us if we just wanted to go with him and work for him on the carnival. We said no. Sandi knew where she was going. I just followed. We ended up in Fargo. We walked up town and went into this little bar to get a drink of water and use the bathroom. We sat down and a couple guys came over to the booth and asked us if we wanted a beer. We said we did not care, sure! So they bought us two.

The bartender did not even ask our age! We were now fifteen and sixteen years old! They asked if we wanted another; we said no. We finished our beers and left. It was now late afternoon. We were hungry. We were trying to decide if the three dollars we had should be used for something to eat or a pack of cigarettes. We decided cigarettes were more important. We walked around town and came to a city park. There were newspapers laying all over the ground there.

We were laying there and a short distance away sat a black man with a long coat on and a fancy hat. Sandi said she thought he was a pimp. I didn't even know what a pimp was! Not long after she told me that, a big car pulled up in front of him sitting on the park bench, and a black woman got out and sat with him. They spoke for a few minutes and she got back into the passenger side and they drove away. The black man stood up and looked our way. Sandi got up and said we'd better go. He started walking toward us. Sandi said if he asked our names don't use our real ones! In case Mom had the police looking for us as runaways.

The black man came up to us. He was very stylish, I thought. He looked of money. He asked us what we were doing and Sandi said we were visiting our aunt. He asked what our names were. Sandi said her name was Amy Sue Allhaven and of course I forgot and said Lisa, Sandi quickly interrupted me and said her name is Heather Ann, her nickname is Lisa. He said, "You can all call me Fox!" and "Hey, if it don't work out at your aunt's and you need a place to crash, I have a real nice pad! I gotta couple bikini's that would fit you both and a big pool you could go swimming." Sandi said no, we had to leave and meet out aunt or she would be mad. So we left "Fox," standing in the park. Thank goodness Sandi was with me, because I believe at fifteen I would have been his lunch. Sandi was wise beyond her years.

As the day grew longer the reality of it struck us! It was now growing dark, no food, no warm clothes, just the clothes on our backs, no place to stay. We walked the streets trying to decide what we were going to do! Where to stay? We found some bushes about two blocks from the main drag of town. We crawled into them, and people walked by on the sidewalk so unaware two young girls were hidden inside! At 11:00 P.M. all we heard were footsteps of passersby, and sirens. It was cold and the bits and pieces of sleep that came were interrupted by dreams of warm blankets. At midnight it started to rain! We huddled trying to keep ourselves warm. By early morning, we had already decided we would go back home. We both drew our little pinkies together and promised each other that we would someday go see the ocean.

We left our bush bed and walked to the freeway and no sooner got to it when a postal truck stopped and gave us a ride right to our driveway! Talk about Jesus watching over us that day! He was with us each step of the way! We crept up the driveway and looked for Mom's car. It was not there! We went in and ate! Each took a blanket and went to the couch and slept. We awoke after about a two-hour nap. We decided we were going to hitchhike back to our sister's house before Mom got home. When we got to our sister's, she asked where we had been! Mom had called the police and reported us as runaways! She called my mom and she came and got us. At the time we thought they were making a big deal out of nothing. But years later, I wondered how we could have ever put Mom through such stress! To not know where her children were! Children can be so unfeeling sometimes. Me and Sandi were seeking adventure! We collected a memory or three, but we also created pain for others in that adventure.

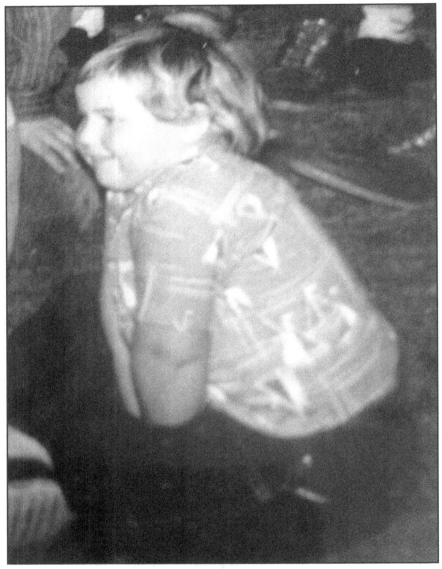

Sandi as a 3-year-old

Oscar as a 4-year-old

Chapter 4

PROVERBS 21:31

Go ahead and prepare for the conflicts, but victory comes from God.

SOON THE FAMILY WAS MOVING AWAY. SANDI QUIT SCHOOL IN her eleventh year. She had turned seventeen in January. It was now the summer of '76. She had gotten a job at the Knute Nelson Memorial Home. We had spread our wings and left home. Jean was living in Long Prairie, Cal in Osakis, Peggy was in Osakis, Connie in Lake Crystal, Kathy in Glencoe, Oscar was in prison in St. Cloud, and Sandi had moved to Alexandria. I went to stay with my sister Kathy and Lonnie was at home with Mom and our stepdad.

Even though I thought we were okay. We never really were. It was winter. We had a very bad blizzard. We had no school that day, weather advisories. We played outside, or tried to it was so bitterly cold, the snow blowing so hard. Ice formed on your eyelashes. No travel was all we heard that day until the TV stood blank and dark because the lights blinked several times and the electric was gone under icy wires. Mom and Dad had drank all day long. By the time supper came that night, they were pretty much inebriated. So Mom dug the candles out and lit them. We brought all the blankets and pillows from our rooms. We were all going to sleep in the living room. Dad had brought the Knipco heater and barbecue grill in. It was like an adventure!

Dad put the Knipco in the kitchen, us kids thought it was exciting, camping in the living room! Dad took the grill down to the basement to the laundry room, opened the window and started the grill, shut the door, and went back upstairs to continue their drinking. Since our stove was electric, he was going to make steaks on the grill. He made the steaks and brought them upstairs. We all ate supper, delicious right off the grill! Us kids went into the living room giggling from excitement of a camping trip upstairs not in our beds!

I just could not settle down. It was exciting! Turning and tossing! My head started hurting so bad! I could actually hear my head pound with each thud I felt. I heard my dad, he was on the phone and he was asking if they could "come to the house." That he thought we were being poisoned by carbon monoxide! He told the police that he had grilled in the basement and that he thought he had enough ventilation with the windows open and the door shut. He told them he was upstairs and he started feeling dizzy and was having chest pains. He went downstairs to the laundry room and opened the door and it was full of smoke. The wind had changed outside and was blowing the smoke right back in. He then came upstairs and called for help. But because all the roads were closed, no one could come!

Mom was yelling about why it was not affecting her! She came in the living room, yelling for us to get outside and in the car! We all got up and my head hurt so bad! Lonnie was behind me and he got as far as the entryway to the kitchen and collapsed on the kitchen floor. Oscar and Sandi helped him out to the car. There we sat, our heads pounding, watching our mom and dad argue about why it happened. They kept all the windows open in the house. Early morning we went back in and it was so frigid cold outside and no warmth inside! It would be twenty-four hours later that the electric would finally come back on. Mom and Dad, I knew loved us, but in their condition, drinking all the time, they were a danger to us and also to themselves! You learned as years back to take care of yourself.

Mom and Dad started drinking a lot harder the end of '75. All day at the bar and all night at home. We would go to town with them and sit in the car all morning and afternoon, while they drank, didn't matter the weather. Later part of the afternoon, they both would come out stumbling drunk to the truck. During the time they were inside, weather got bad and it was a blizzard out, no travel the radio would say. The temperatures with the wind chill was forty-two below zero! But you could never make them leave till they were ready.

The wind and snow were blowing so hard. We got a mile and a half away from home and they decided to start arguing about who can drive better! Mom reaches over and yanks the steering wheel and we went sliding in the ditch! And we sat there, no more fighting, just sitting. Pretty quick, Dad said we were to stay in the truck and he would walk to the neighbor's for help. They lived about a quarter mile back from where we were.

As soon as he left and started walking, Mom said that he would start drinking over there and not come back. She jumped out of the truck and said she was not waiting for him! Me and Lonnie watched her walking away. We looked at each other. Should we or shouldn't we? We both got out, the icy wind hitting our faces. We caught up to Mom and each took an arm. Soon she was yelling at us to let her go! She wanted to lay down; she was tired!

"Leave me alone!" We were about a quarter mile from the house, I took off running to get my uncles to come help us!

I pounded on their door and said, "Please help! Dad is walking and Mom doesn't want to keep walking!" I ran back out to meet Lonnie and Mom. They were just coming up the driveway. We got inside. My lungs hurt so bad from breathing in all that cold, icy air while running. Lonnie's hands were frozen. He ran warm water on them in the bathroom, and cried from the pain. Twenty minutes later, Dad came with the neighbor.

He came in and said, "I thought I told you to stay in the truck!" His ears were bleeding from severe frostbite. He walked in the bathroom where me and Lonnie were. Lonnie still crying from the pain. Dad left and came back with two hot brandies and told us that this would warm us up! How funny, that alcohol had caused all this. Yet, he was offering it to us for comfort.

The drinking grew worse, if that were possible. Mom would come home at night and Dad would be passed out across the bed. Soon a man would pick her up and they would leave. I would go upstairs after she left and go to my mom's bedroom door and there Dad would be, passed out, unaware that his wife had left. I would be afraid to go to sleep. They fought all the time. My mom would grab forks at suppertime as we ate and stick them up to my dad's throat as she had him backed against the wall. Me and Lonnie would struggle to get them out of her hand and get them apart. Then she would rake her nails down the side of his face, before you could get them separated. Leaving a path of blood where her nails had traveled.

One evening I came awake with a start! I had heard something, maybe a bang or thump. It sounded like it came from the garage. I did hear something! There it was again! I took two steps at a time up the stairs! Opened the door that led to the garage and my dad had mom by the throat and was trying to shove her under the car! I yelled, "What do you think you're doing!" He said he was trying to help her up, she had fallen. I was so scared for my mom. I was scared she would fall asleep or pass out with a cigarette and start herself on fire. I was afraid of her driving. I rode many times with her so she would not run off the road or fall asleep and have an accident. To this day I am in terror to ride with anyone who has been drinking. In the summer of '75, my mom tried committing suicide. She took a bunch of pills and locked herself in her sewing room. I had not even realized that she had until Dad came yelling at us while we were watching TV, saying we drove her to it. He spent all that day with her. Walking with her, keeping her awake. We were quiet as little church mice. Not knowing what we had done to her that made her not want to live anymore with us. We loved her!

Me and Lonnie spent most of our time skipping school. Mom and Dad caught us skipping and they had us get in the truck. They were both drunk, and Mom was yelling and saying it was all my fault. That Lonnie would never think of skipping school, that I was the troublemaker and put the idea in his head. I went to stay with my dad and his wife in St. Cloud. I stayed there for only a couple of months. I think Mom sent me there because I was hopeless. I hadn't seen my dad since I was six and was now soon to be fifteen. She packed my clothes and I went to a man I never knew and believed he never wanted me. I could not carry on a conversation with him. I didn't know who he was. I stayed to myself. I tried going into alternative school, which I liked.

One day I came home from school and my bags were packed. I asked where I was going and he said, "You're going back to your mother's."

I asked, "Why, what did I do?" It brought back childhood memories of my aunt Ginny hitting me and me never knowing what I had done wrong.

He said, "You don't want to be here anyway!" So I was taken back to Mom. I knew this man, who was my dad, hated me! He did not want me around. I never saw him again until he was in the hospital ten years later.

Chapter 5

HEBREWS 12:11

Being punished isn't enjoyable while it is happening—it hurts! But afterwards we can see the results, a quiet growth in grace and character.

LONNIE AND I WOULD TAKE ALL THE ALCOHOL OUT OF THE LIQUOR cabinet. We would drink it, get drunk, and be sick, just so they could not. They would never say anything about it being gone. They would just replenish what was gone. Nothing was ever getting fixed, because no one was ever around to start fixing. Mom was never coming home till late at night. I would get ready for bed and close my door. I would hear my dad walking upstairs. He would come to the stairs and whistle and call my name: "Lisa!"

I would say to myself, "Please don't come down here!" Then I held my breath till I heard his footsteps recede away, pretty soon the footsteps would return with the same whistle and calling my name. The next day my brother put a lock on my door and I felt so much safer. At least he could not get me! A few days later, Mom was home and I got the courage to tell her what he was doing. She got angry and said I was trying to cause trouble.

In November of '76, we had a family get-together for Thanksgiving. I had been at my sister Kathy's going to school. I had not seen Sandi for ages it seemed. Sandi came in and she was so pretty! She was the tallest of us girls.

She had cut her long hair short. She always had so much energy. Mom and our dad were drinking; they were drunk. As the night wore on, they started to argue. And soon everyone was leaving. We went back to Glencoe and I started making some friends and we did what young kids did, drank and went to parties. I stole my sister's boyfriend's car, hit a bunch of mailboxes with it and lied to try to get out of it. I started work at a drive-in. And started going out to parties with a guy named "Goggles." I was going on sixteen, and he was twenty-five. Took him back home to meet my mom and dad. They seemed to like him. When we got back to my sister's. I went out with one of my friends and I caught him with another girl. So we broke up. He would try to talk to me, but I wanted nothing to do with him. All I wanted was to party and have a good time. I was, I guess, having fun. But it would be my problem, the same problem my parents had.

Chapter 6

PHILIPPIANS 4:1–4

Fix your thoughts on what is true and good and right. Think about things that are pure and lovely, and dwell on the fine, good things in others. Think about all you can praise God for and good things in others. Think about all you can praise God for and be glad about. Keep putting into practice all you learned from me and saw me doing, and God of peace will be with you.

AROUND DECEMBER 7, 1976. MOM CALLED MY SISTERS AND asked if we had seen Sandi. Kathy said no. Mom said no one had seen or heard from her since December 3. I thought maybe she had gone to California without me! I was worried. It wasn't like her to leave me and just go without telling me what her plans were. Mom called us later that night and told us that all her belongings were in her apartment. Her coat, gloves, cap, and purse. She had not taken anything with her. She said she reported her missing. I came home to be with Mom. To support her. And came home to a lot of crazy behavior! Mom and I went to the police station. Mom was asked a lot of questions. I suppose everyone becomes a person of interest in a disappearance. I asked Mom why that was. She said that when someone in your family comes up missing, they always question the family members first, because they are the last ones most likely that have seen them. I knew Sandi had to be alive; she could not be dead! She just left, maybe she had to leave!

The police had taken all the evidence from her apartment and they told my mom she could go and move Sandi's things out. Her apartment was on the main level of a two-story house. There were people that were living upstairs. We stepped up to Sandi's door. I did not want my first visit to her home to be like this. Sandi had been in this apartment for three days. She had just moved from a previous apartment, into this house with a friend that she worked with. Mom turned the door handle, the light shone across the room. As you entered, you were in her living room. This was Sandi's home! I had never been here before. Couch, television, stereo, bookshelf—all the things a person would have to make a home. Perhaps gifts from our mom. Off to the side of the living room to the left was a door that was closed and next to that a bathroom. Straight ahead from where we stood, you could see into the dark unlit kitchen. Off to the far right was a bedroom.

We stood, we stood, and we stood. We looked for hopes, for possibilities, for Sandi. All that came back to hit us in the stomach was emptiness. Nothing, just an empty, silent apartment. Once lived in, with stereo music, her laughter, of life, but no more. Mom stepped forward and I followed behind. I wondered why I was here. As she headed to the only door that was ajar. The bathroom seemed almost brighter, a happier place, with the light-colored walls. I could see little spots on the sink. I wondered for a brief second if this is where a sixteen-year-old should be? Did I want to know what had happened here? Or stay in my make-believe world, where everything was going to be okay and a reason for everything. Mom, turned and walked out and took ahold of the handle to the door that was closed. Hesitating, briefly, as if to renew her strength, Mom slowly turned the handle and moved into the room. And there stood. Not believing what was before my eyes!

Sandi's room was very bright, as energetic as her personality. A beam of the sun shone through the two windows she had there. There were boxes, several gone through as I imagined her unpacking, to start a new season of her life. Her bed was against the wall as you faced straight into her room, a dresser sat against the opposite wall across from her bed. A closet on the same wall as the door. My eyes scanned the room and stopped at her bed. My eyes caught the spatters of blood on the wall and the windowsill. I followed them down to her mattress, bare, with no sheets now. There were spatters of blood and a big circle of blood that had soaked the side of her mattress and ran onto the floor. We stepped in ignoring the blood, looked in boxes, trying to find answers. We slowly got up from our crouched positions and walked out of this room of terror and shut the door. We walked into the kitchen and went through drawers. What were we looking for? Against the wall in the kitchen was another closed door. Mom opened it and the smell of mildew hit us in the face. It was dark, and damp. Mom turned the light on and I squinted at the brightness of the bulb.

Along the wall a row of fruit jars and some boxes sat on the dirt floor and on the concrete ledge. Sandi's blood was on the fruit jars and had run down the side of the wall and onto the boxes and floor. We never said a word to each other. We walked in silence. Our minds envisioning our own horrors. My sister's blood had seeped through her whole home! Violence had not left a room untouched! We took all her things back to Mom's. As we left I thought this house should be burned down! On our way home, we stopped at the police station. I knew that my best friend would never grace us with her presence. That she fought for her life against a vicious animal. And that she was no more a part of our world.

We went to Chief George McKay's office. And he asked who Amy Sue Allhaven was? We did not know, and we told him. He said that he found a piece of paper in her room and that name was written on it. If he could find out who she was, he would like to talk to her. It would be a couple of weeks before I would remember who she was. It haunted me. I had heard the name before. It was familiar. Several weeks after Sandi's disappearance, I was once again struggling with the familiarity of this name Amy Sue Allhaven! Then one day a light came on! I knew who she was. She was Sandi! The same name she used when she and I had left to go to California. I cried, I should have remembered. Sandi had never lost the dream she still had.

That day we left the house and talked with George McKay. I asked him if he thought she suffered. There was no questions anymore about her still being alive. We all knew she was not. He said he believed she died right away. But I would not! I wondered for many years now unto this day what events transpired and how she died. I knew with the amount of blood in each room there had to be more. I had to find out!

LISA L COLSEN

My Mom and Sandi

Chapter 7

1 CORINTHIANS 13:13

There are three things that remain—faith, hope, and love—and the greatest of these is love.

THUS BEGINS THE SEARCH, THE HORRORS, THE NIGHTMARES. that came out of the vicious murder of my sister. The spiral, spin of alcohol, anger, and sorrow. This person took the life of my sister and hid her from us. Not only took her! But also my family!

December of '76, we as a family started searching for our missing family member. Where to start? Who knew, anywhere that looked suspicious. Old buildings, mounds of dirt, in ditches. Our vehicle would come to a screeching halt and out we would go into the cold December winter, to bend to our knees. Feel the cold, wetness of snow seep through the jeans of your knees. Feel the ache of your hands as you dug into the hardness of the earth. To see if that is where our Sandi lay. Every day for four months, unless storms brewed. That was our day. Not playing football, not watching TV, not being the typical teen-age child, but looking for our buried treasure. My ears can still hear the crunching of the snow as we went to another empty building, to another mound of dirt covered with snow.

Fear! Not wanting to be the one to end the dream, but yet wanting her found. Hating yourself for having such selfish feelings. Mom and Dad were drinking all the time now. Morning till the search would stop at night, too dark to see. Then return trip home, more drinking, more arguing, on where to search, where to look next. I would go down to the room that me and Sandi had shared. Where we shared secrets, future, hopes and all our dreams. I was alone with my sorrow. No one to share my fears. Silence, only met me there. The echo of her laughter, gone. I cried for Sandi, the life we had as small children and how it had ended for her in such a violent way. Why did life seem so cruel to us? I cried for my mom. At her loss of her child, of the alcoholism she had, that compounded all her feelings. So she could never really come to terms with this sadness in a healthy way.

I sat on our bed and prayed to a God I did not know. Asking him why? Why was it not me that this happened to? I was the troublemaker! I was the shy one! Why her! She was so full of energy. Her laughter was so contagious. A soft, inner voice came to me, *"She would have felt the same, if it would have been you."* I knew God was someone out there. But that was all. Everything that had happened to us in our lives, I believed he didn't care for us much.

We spent a great deal of time in bars, those four months. We would plan another search over cocktails when we arose in the morning. There was a guy the police suspected of killing Sandi. He was staying with his parents in Parkers Prairie. Mom and Dad would have their friends with them. I guess at the time, we did not call them friends as much as called them our posse of searchers. Of course most of them were alcoholics also. Because your posse has to be just like you, they have to understand you. On a cold December afternoon, Mom and Dad and our posse spent a few hours at a bar in Urbank. We left there in a very angry mood, after a day of unsuccessful searching.

We made a trip to Parkers Prairie. It was dark by now. We parked in front of this guy's parent's trailer house. His parents owned the trailer court there. They all stumbled out of the car, up to the trailer house door. Dad had a gun that he had started carrying ever since Sandi disappeared. He knocked on the door. There was no reply. Dad knocked just a little bit harder and the door opened just a crack! The guy stood in shadow and stepped into the light that shined from the street, for only a brief second. This was the first time I had ever seen him, this guy, who they were saying murdered my sister! Everything slowed to a snail's pace! The guy's features entered my brain, as though I were a computer, taking in important data.

This guy stood a stately, six feet tall, he was slim, he I guessed was about 175 pounds. He had a glare of reddish colored, fuzzy hair. He had blue eyes, that showed fear. A mustache also to match the shock of fuzzy reddish hair. His tone of skin seemed to have a reddish gleam to it. I wondered, in my mind if it was his natural tone or if it was lack of sleep that made his appearance seem so strained and so unnatural to me. In those few seconds, things began to change from slow motion and went to flying sparks of electricity! He opened the door, a bit wider, Dad asked his name, he replied. Dad said, he was Sandi's father. There came no reply to this statement. He brought up his hand in a feeble attempt to slam the door quickly in our faces. In that shocking instant, Dad put his foot in the door and stopped the door from closing, and raised the pistol and aimed it directly at this guy's face. He just stood there, he did not run away. He just stood there, holding the door. The thought that seeped into my mind at that instant was of one rinsing the mud off their hands. The redness of his skin just seeped out of him and he went to a deathly white! As if someone had poured bleach on a dirty sheet. There was no color to this man except the shocking red hair atop his head.

Dad's cousin took hold of him and pulled him back and Dad began to sob, he cried, "She was not mine, but she was mine! In my heart, she was mine!" It seemed time stopped, as we stood on that cold winter's night, trying to convince him not to lower himself to what we considered this guy to be. The guy just stood there as if in shock. Just as quickly as he realized my dad had been removed from the door. The door was slammed shut! The lock turned and snapped shut. There went the chance at being the animal that he was and avenging our sister and daughter's death on the one who so boldly took the breath from her!

Mom stood there crying as we turned and slowly walked to the car and back to the bar. We sat there, them with their drinks. Dad repeating as he pointed his right hand into the fashion of a gun. "I had him right here!" Several days later, we were back in Parkers Prairie, driving past his parent's place again. We left and headed to the Old Mill Bar in Urbank. This guy's brother lived there on a farm on the outskirts of town. It had a lot of woods and a very long driveway. The door to the bar opened and we turned to see who had come in. There stood a sheriff from Ottertail County. He scanned the room, spotted us and came over to our table. The sheriff was kind and considerate. He knew our desperation in our search. But he also had his job to do.

He explained to us that he would have to escort us out of Ottertail County, and if we did not comply, he would have to arrest us for harassment. This guy was, he said, in fear of his life! What about my sister! Did he not think for one minute maybe she had been in fear of her life also! When she was fighting him off her, did he not comprehend she had been more than afraid for her life! Was he so self-centered as not to see how ridiculous that sounded to us! Coming from the one who brutally killed her, so animal-like! Fear for his life didn't matter to us! We, as Sandi's family, knew what every kind of fear was! We lived with fear, tasted fear, smelled fear, and went to bed with fear as our constant companion, now going on a month!

We left town with the sheriff following behind us until we were out of Ottertail County. Soon we pulled back into our driveway. I slowly walked downstairs to what used to be our room and I cried in confusion and anger and sadness. This guy took my sister's life! But he also was taking my whole family with her too! He was taking the safety and security of my home! The home that we had longed for all our young lives to have! He had the power as long as he had my sister. He could bend us and break our mind, our hearts! He had this power as long as he had my sister!

I drifted off into restless sleep of dreams that would not end. A red-haired stranger, with shiny white teeth, laughing and laughing and his repeated words, "You can't catch me!" Sitting straight up in bed trying to catch my breath and waiting for the thud of my heart pounding to subside and slowly fade from my ears. My brain slowed to a more rational thinking. My eyes adjusting to the glow of the light I left on in case Sandi would return to our room and not be able to see where she was going. My source of light, my ray of hope that maybe she still inhabited this earth somewhere.

These are pictures of the posse and police department conducting searches in a drainage pipe and also in an area of woods.

Chapter 8

ISAIAH 40:6–8

The voice says, "Shout!"

"What shall I shout?" I asked.

"Shout that man is like grass that dies away, and all his beauty fades like dying flowers. The grass withers, the flowers fade beneath the breath of God. And so it is with fragile man. The grass withers, the flowers fade, but the word of our God shall stand forever.

IT WAS QUIET NOW IN THE HOUSE. I THOUGHT, EVERYONE HAD either fallen asleep or passed out after the nights drinking and arguing, the untold horrors they believed they could drown away in a bottle. I slowly walked up the stairs, realizing it was peaceful, no loud clatter of bottles and pots and pans, from a hurried meal. To the clank of bottles meeting glass. No loud talk and no swearing spoken out in hate. Nothing but silence, complete calmness. As I stood at the top of the stairs, a small light burned on the stove. Wait, I thought I heard something. I did, a small wail perhaps from a baby? "We have no baby here." I walked through the kitchen and the wails were louder, though they sounded muffled, as if a hand had covered its sound. So it would not wake anyone that might be asleep.

I felt a great compassion for this wailing. It sounded so strained and lost and afraid. The need for me to find and care for this broken wail drew me closer to the sound from where it came. It sounded like it was coming from the bathroom. The door was closed, but I knew the crying was within that room. I opened the door without hesitation. It was totally dark, except for the few rays of moonlight filtering through the window. I stood at the open door and my mind did not register anything. The wailing ceased into a jagged, mournful, strained sound of small gasps as if the person were trying to hide itself from being found there in the dark. A sound of someone that had everything torn from their soul and were trying to hang on to this world.

My eyes adjusted to the darkness and there in the far corner on the floor, crouched my mom. Her face was strained in pain and wet with her tears. She was looking up at me with such desperation and torment on her face. I flew to meet her there on the floor in the corner of the bathroom and I put my arms around her and we rocked and cried and rocked. She repeated over and over to me, "What am I gonna do?" The words still echo in my heart today. I held her as her body trembled and shook, and I realized as I sat and cried for my lost sister, that I also cried for my mom. I could never fathom the cries that came from so deep within my mom's soul. She cried for her baby, the child that she bore into this world and had given life to. We sat there on that cold bathroom floor till the wee hours of a dawning new day, till she felt she could stand another. And the edge of insanity left those eyes of blue.

It is January, soon it will be Sandi's eighteenth birthday. It is hard to believe that we are still looking and time that I thought should stand still is forever going on! Time was not being fair to us! My brother Cal came over and again we started our fruitless searching. We stopped at the Urbank bar to warm up. We came up emptyhanded again. By eight o'clock that night, Mom, Dad, and Cal had had a lot to drink. We finally called it a night and went home. Upon our return, more drinks were drunk as Mom prepared supper. There were conversations about running out of places to look and to go back and look at the places we had looked in the beginning. My brother made a comment that maybe something had gotten missed in our previous searches.

As nerves were raw from the fruitless searching, lack of sleep, and too much drinking, Mom directed her anger and frustration at him with very hurtful words. She yelled, that he was not searching for Sandi with his heart! My mouth went open as I realized what she had said to him in her moment of hurt. The kind of pain she as a mother felt. My reaction was slow compared to my brother's. He jumped like a jack-in-the-box from the chair he sat on at the table. I tried to get there before they did anything that they would never be able to undo! I was too slow. I heard the *crack* of his hand against her face and her head reeled to the side from the force and her false teeth sailed to clatter against the cupboard. He had a hold of her by the front of her blouse. As I cleared my head at the absolute horror I was seeing, I quickly stepped to them and tried to get in between them. I yelled at them! I could not understand how they could be attacking each other so viciously, when we were all we had!

I yelled again, "What're you doing? Do you see yourselves! Sandi would be terribly disappointed in both of you! Fighting and saying such mean things, and hurtful things, blaming each other! If she knew what was going on here, in this family, she would not even want to be a part of it!"

They were both crying. Cal slowly let loose of Mom's clothes and returned to his place at the table, as the tears softly ran down his cheeks. He whispered over and over to me, "How could she, how could she?" I slumped down into the chair next to him as Mom bent and picked up her false teeth, where they had landed and quickly ran into the bathroom sobbing. Which one? Which one needed me the most? Who should I go and give myself to? Which one needed my hand to pull them back once more from the edge of insanity? I decided my brother needed what little I had left to give. I would give everything I had remaining in me to comfort the horrible words our mom had spoken to her son. He looked at me and he said, "My heart is in it, Lisa, my heart is in it!" I told him not to take Mom serious, that it was the booze and all the emotions she was feeling, so she struck out at him because he was there. He walked out of our house that night, not to speak or go see Mom again for two years.

I could not believe what was happening to my family. Their minds were always dulled by the amount of alcohol they kept in their bodies, so they didn't have to feel anything.

Chapter 9

2 Corinthians 13:1

This is the third time I am coming to visit you. The scriptures tell us that if two or three seen a wrong, it must be punished, this is my third warning, as I come now for this visit.

WE WERE BACK IN PARKERS PRAIRIE, AT THE BAR FOR WHAT seemed like the millionth time. It was now January 21—Sandi's birthday! She would be turning eighteen years old. Mom and Dad and the posse were once again drinking and we were warming up from our latest journey into another unknown woods.

I walked outside to get away from the clanking glasses, the drinking, the smoke, and all the sorrow of everything. There right beside me was a pay phone, "Oh, do I dare!" I stood and stared at the black pay phone, an idea formed in my mind. I took the wet soggy phone book that hung there by a chain and looked under, Harley Hallen Sr. and PRESTO! There it was, his dad's name and even his address! Right there! I stood there and questioned myself a few seconds, the whys and the why nots. The pros outweighed the cons. I slowly picked up the ice-cold receiver. Crammed my hand into my jeans pocket. Produced a nice warm dime and let it drop with a clatter into the slot and dialed the number with cold stubby, shaky fingers.

It rang once, "Oh God, let me have the courage!" It rang twice. "Please don't let me hang up before they answer!" It rang a third time.

"Hello."

"Yes, is this Harley, or is he there?"

"Just a minute, please." I told myself don't hang up before he says hello. To my surprise there came a voice on the other end. He sounded tired and worn.

"Hi!" I replied back. As if to an old friend. Again he repeated hi. I asked him, "How are you sleeping?" He did not reply. I said, "You know who this is, don't you?"

He simply replied, "No."

I said, "This is Sandi." His breath caught.

Then quickly he said, "But you can't!" Then slammed the receiver down and its echo of a dial tone lingered in my ear.

I slowly hung the receiver back in its unyielding arm and I turned and smiled to myself and said, "GOTCHA!" I looked up to the heavens and whispered, "Thank you." He had confessed to me in a two-minute conversation, in three small words, *But you can't!* In his mind it could never be Sandi. He knew she was dead! And he had done it! Now all we had to do was get the best piece of the puzzle—Sandi. Then we could try to heal all the broken hearts that this one man created.

I wonder at how desperate a person will get in their loss. To go to such extremes, to call the killer and try to get him to admit something, or my dad going to physically hurt him. Mom and Dad had their alcohol. Perhaps I had my own form of revenge. To torment the killer. No, I never went back in the bar to shout my victory I felt in those words he spoke. I sat in the corner of the booth and watched my parents destroying themselves. I kept secret, never to tell anyone except for you right here and right now. I thought about Sandi, that for once she was not alone. I connected with her. I would be the one this time to hang my arm over her shoulder and say, "It will be okay, Sandi. They will find you soon."

I would be where she was in my heart. I would sit in spirit beside her. Where she was, I would spread my warmth across her body as a blanket. So she would not be cold at night. I would be her light so she would not lay in darkness. I would be with her until someone came to get her. I was there in her aloneness, it was my loneliness. Her pain in not being found was my pain. Her wanting to be set free, was my wanting her to be set free. Her justice was my justice. Her hopes of us not giving up the search were my hopes of never giving up.

The angel of mercy that was sent to us by God. To make all the wrongs right and to make sure everything came into place was Chief George McKay. The greatest of men here on earth. I will probably never meet anyone ever like him again. He was a once-in-a-lifetime angel.

I wrote this as a fifteen-year-old child. Not really knowing what the investigation was all about. That part of it all did not seem important at the time. Just the loss of her. All I knew was that my best friend was gone, and life at my house was never the same after the tragic loss of Sandi. Yes, we went on living, but the brutality of the world stayed forever with us.

So, I go back forty-five years into the death of my sister. To search for the answers my heart seeks and has yearned for these many years. To know what happened and why she lost her beautiful life that night. I dig back into old interviews of the witnesses. Court transcripts and newspaper articles. To find the reasons for this that still haunt me today. I knew the hell of those four months! The terrors of the times I used to call them. What occurred during Sandi's last days of her young life. I have come to realize the brutality that envelopes this world of ours. To know and understand that humans can be so vicious. You can succumb to that hatred or you can say that is beneath me, I am better than that. To hate the act but forgive the person. Once you know that truth that real act of violence. To wonder if you could forgive that person, for the actions he made that forever altered our lives and his. And yes, maybe I can.

The apartment Sandi lived in at 1115 Hawthorne St, where she was murdered.

Chapter 10

PSALMS 73:24

You will keep on giving me all my life with your wisdom and counsel, and afterwards receive me into the glories.

O N DECEMBER 1, SANDI MOVED INTO THE HAWTHORNE apartment. A two bedroom. She was moving from another apartment, in with a friend she had known from her work. They were going to share the rent there. So it would be more affordable for two young girls just starting out. Mom was helping her move her things into Tammy's place, since she already lived there. On the first, Sandi and Tammy went to work and got off at three in the afternoon. And caught a ride with a friend of Tammy's home. When they arrived, there was a guy parked in the driveway in a truck, waiting for Tammy. An old friend of Tammy's. She and Sandi got out of the car and he met them by the car. Tammy introduced him to Tammy's friend and Sandi as Harley.

Tammy and her friend (his name was Terry Lion), were talking about a date they were to have that night. Sandi said that Mom was coming to get her to go home for the weekend. Sandi went in and started painting her bedroom and hanging pictures. Tammy and Harley Hallen Jr., or as some called him simply Art, left and went to Hardee's to catch up on what each other had been up to. They talked and he said he was just back from New York and he was looking for a job. She asked him if he wanted to move in with them for a while till he found a job. He could share the rent, so they went to the apartment to talk with Sandi about his living there and she agreed. That evening Tammy left on her date at around eight. Sandi was laying on the couch reading a book waiting for Mom to pick her up. Harley was in his bedroom.

Tammy came home around eight thirty, Saturday morning. She didn't see Sandi there and assumed Mom had come and picked her up. When she came into the apartment, she noticed Sandi's coat, hat, and mittens laying on the end of the couch. So, she glanced into her dark bedroom and she was not there. A bit later she was going to the bathroom and she noticed little droplets of blood in the sink and on some makeup containers, so she came out and asked Harley where the blood came from in the bathroom. He said he cut himself shaving. She asked about Sandi on and off all day. He said when he got home from the "Barn" (a local popular bar with the young people), he came in went to the bathroom and went to bed.

Tammy said on the fifth, Harley told her he had gotten a phone call at about nine o'clock in the morning from a girl he thought was Sandi. She asked for Tammy, he told her, she wasn't there, she said, "Well, tell her I am taking off with a girlfriend and I am not coming back!" To get rid of her things. Tammy said she got mad and threw a fit! Said, "Well, my God! Why should I have to pay all these bills! Why is Sandi doing this!" Tammy said she called Mom on Tuesday, because the head nurse at Knute Nelson Memorial Home wanted to know why Sandi had not shown up for her scheduled shift. Tammy said she got a little worried, with Harley telling her about the phone call and everything just seemed strange. So she decided to call Mom. She asked Mom if Sandi was there? Mom said no. She asked Mom if she had seen her at all over the weekend? Mom said no. Tammy said, "I thought you were going to pick her up after work?" Mom said she had forgotten.

After this call on the seventh, Mom called all of us kids to see if we had seen Sandi. She called our dad in St. Cloud. She called hospitals, funeral homes, and no one had a Sandi Karnes. So Mom called the police. Mom drove to Alexandria and she drove by the apartment. She saw a truck sitting there in the driveway. So she drove around the block and parked. She knocked on the door and Harley opened the door. She told him she wanted to look through Sandi's things. Mom said she had never had seen him before that day. She did know that Harley was living there, because the day she helped Sandi move in, there was a black dog there and Mom asked Sandi whose dog that was and Sandi said it was Tammy's friend's dog.

Mom said, "Well, what is it doing here?"

"Well," Sandi said, "he is living here." Mom told Harley she was Sandi's mom and that she had reported her missing and wanted to see if she could figure out what she was wearing. Mom went to her bedroom and Harley told her that all her bedding was gone, that she must have just taken off with somebody. He said this five or six times. Mom was looking at Sandi's things and everywhere she went to look, Harley was there over her shoulder looking too. When Mom checked everything, she called the police. Mom said Harley appeared nervous and kept walking around and saying it was cold in there. When she would ask him questions, like where had Sandi gone, Harley told her that Sandi had called him on Saturday. He said that the girl said that she was leaving and that she would explain to him later.

When Mom called the police, Carl Blomglen arrived. Mom told him everything that was going on. He started looking around and after that told them not to touch anything. Mom told the deputy that when she arrived, Sandi's bedroom door had been closed and she had opened it to look in there. The only people there at the time Officer Blomglen arrived were Mom and Harley. He took all the information from Mom about Sandi. Deputy Blomglen notified the city police, and made contact with the crime bureau. Officer Blomglen looked in Sandi's room and also the living room. He did not speak with Harley. Soon Lamont Mounds arrived from the City Police Department. Then Officer Blomglen started looking around in the house just to see if he could find any evidence of any kind that would indicate Sandi's whereabouts.

At this time Mom and Harley were kept outside. Officer Blomglen went back into the bedroom, then the kitchen. He found a door, which he thought was just a pantry, but ended up leading to the basement. It was a small basement, under Sandi's bedroom. When Officer Blomglen went down into the basement. There were cardboard boxes and fruit jars. The boxes were against the concrete wall on the dirt floor and the jars were on a concrete ledge above them. He noticed a red blotch. The fruit jars had been spattered by this red substance also. To Officer Blomglen it appeared to be blood. He gave an estimate of how much blood he found, and in his opinion it was about a pint or sixteen ounces. Officer Blomglen then called for Officer Mounds to come to the basement. He showed him what he had found. Showed him how it had dripped through the floor. He looked up at the ceiling to see where it came from. He saw run marks, dripping down out of the floor and down the floor joist or two-by-sixes.

They then went back upstairs into Sandi's room to see if they could locate the area where this had come from. They did not find anything. They went into the bathroom to see if they could see anything there. They did not notice anything in there either, so they went back down to the basement, and they pinpointed why they thought it came from Sandi's bedroom. They went back up into Sandi's bedroom again and they got down on their hands and knees and looked on the floor. They noticed an area on the floor that had been cleaned really well. The water had gone down in between the wood on the floor. They noticed cracks in the boards.

Then Officer Benner came in. He had been called from the police department. Officer Blomglen got down and looked right in the cracks of those boards. He could see the red substance in between the cracks. It had been dried. Deputy Mounds took a flashlight and checked the cracks along the floor. They found the red substance had run down at least three boards for eighteen inches. He guessed that approximately three quarters of a pint to a pint of this substance was in the basement. He told Deputy Blomglen that they needed to get ahold of the Crime Agent Bureau. So Deputy Blomglen called the sheriff's office and checked to see if Gary Neilsen was in the area.

Then Deputy Mounds started talking with Harley Hallen. He asked Harley how many people had been there since December third. Harley said, Terry Lion had been there on Friday night, Saturday night, and on Monday night. And also a man from up North that had come in on Sunday afternoon and left for Florida, but Harley said he could not recall his name. Deputy Mounds asked Harley when he had last seen Sandi? He said about eight o'clock December third. Harley said at the time, she was laying on the couch, reading a book. She was wearing jeans, or he said, dressed in jeans. He was going to show Deputy Mounds the book she was reading and Mounds told him to leave the book where it was. Mounds asked Harley where he had been on Friday. Harley said that he had went to the "Barn." Harley said he left at around eight or eight fifteen. Soon after this, Deputy Warner came and Harley Hallen left with him.

Harley Hallen Jr. the man who murdered our sister.

Chapter 11

2 Chronicles 6:31

Then they will reverence you forever, and will continually walk where you tell them to go.

Deputy Mounds then continued his search of the house. He recovered a pillowcase against the east wall in Sandi's room. He took the pillowcase and also the purse he had been given. He put the purse inside the pillowcase and took them with him when he left. He looked at the pillowcase in the office under close light and found little red specks all over it. Than later he locked away the pillowcase, later giving it to Terry Labber, from the Minnesota Bureau of Criminal Apprehension. Deputy Mounds returned to the apartment to further investigate the condition of the floor in Sandi's bedroom. Terry Labber and another agent from the Crime Bureau were there at the time the crime lab worked on the blood splatters in the room. Afterwards he removed the floor, where the scrapes were and also where the red substance was. What they found underneath the floor, was a subfloor with a sleeper. That is what carpenters call it. A shim underneath between the floors. More like a lath for shimming purpose. We found a red substance along those boards.

When you find blood at the scene of a crime, first you have to classify the blood. The blood is classified into different systems which are, the systems set up on a national level. If they give a blood type here and the blood typing is done somewhere else in the nation, they know that they're talking about the same thing.

Terry Labber went to Sandi's apartment on the eighth. He was with Dan Bergstand and Walter Roads. The home was empty upon their arrival except for the guard out front. The first thing they did was look around to see if there was a good place to set up their equipment. They started processing at the front door. What they were looking for were bloodstains or any hairs or fibers or anything that would be present. In the area between the door and screen, on the inside of the screen, there were some apparent bloodstains. These were in the form of a smear or smudge marks. The blood that was enough to remove for blood grouping tests was located on the outside of the main door. These bloodstains were circled and then they were removed onto cloth so they were taken to the lab for blood grouping tests.

They then proceeded to go in a direction towards what would be, what he called the hallway. It really was not much of a hallway, but it was an area between the bathroom and what was Sandi's bedroom. There were bloodstains, some small blood spots on the living room carpet. These were removed. The couch sat right on the edge by the outside door. So approximately a foot away from the couch, there were two or three blood droppings. These were removed for testing. There was blood on the wall, which would be next to the entrance to the hallway with the bathroom on one side and bedroom on the other. There was a small spot of blood on the wall there.

In the door casing on the right-hand side as you are facing the hallway, going up the wall for an area of about two feet—there were bloodstains on the actual wood casings. These were taken for testing. There were also small flakes of blood, possibly that had fallen off the casing or from some other area that were laying on the carpet near the wall, little crusts of blood. These were all collected. He then noticed a clump of hair with apparent tissue attached to it. It was a 1/4 of an inch by 1/8 of an inch thick; this had possibly 30, 40, to 50 hairs coming out of the clump. He located that clump of tissue in the hallway up against the wall on the far side of the hallway.

Then he moved to Sandi's room. Labber noticed that there were two areas on the floor that apparently had been scraped of paint. The paint had been scraped away in a couple different areas of the floor. Upon closer inspection, these areas, indicated that blood ran down between the boards where the scrapings occurred. He removed blood from in between the boards. It was noticed that there were bloodstains on the mattress. The stains were in the form of real small spatters. They were on the lower edge of the mattress. The mattress was hanging over the box spring about four or five inches, and on the lower edge of the mattress there were small splatters.

So the mattress was turned over and two more blood spots or stains were noted on the mattress. When they entered the room, the mattress was in this particular location. It was hanging over the box spring and there was not any apparent bloodstaining on the mattress. When the mattress was turned over, along the edge, it was noted that there was several spatters along the edge of the mattress approximately two inches to either seam. This area of mattress was cut out and taken to the lab.

The room was examined for other areas of bloodstaining. Also there were numerous articles against the far wall of Sandi's room, clothing, boxes, these types of items. They went through the boxes and articles of clothing to see if any of these articles had bloodstaining. In the corner there were some cushions piled up. Also some clothing and boxes with clothing piled on the boxes. He found a purse and some letters and papers. These were gone through. There was bloodstaining on the purse, on the handle of the purse, and on three articles of clothing—a T-shirt, a dish cloth, and a terrycloth type top. They were taken to the lab. These were all found against the far wall in Sandi's room.

He noticed also through his examination, areas of bloodstaining on the wall, blood spatters underneath the windowsill and on the window. He started on the wall. There were only about two small blood spatters. These had apparently come from the direction, hit just behind the mattress so it cleared the mattress and hit the wall, so they were actually covered by the mattress if you stood back in this area. You could not see them unless you were right up close and looking at an angle over the mattress. The window had numerous small blood spatters—approximately fifteen to twenty of them. The windowsill came out, and underneath the windowsill there were numerous spatters. The spatters indicated they came from an area below the windowsill because they were underneath the windowsill.

It is consistent that the spatters came from the mattress. He was unable to tell whether the mattress had been turned over. So when stains came to the mattress from on top, it is possible they could have come from an area between the mattress and window. More likely that the spatters came from underneath the mattress. The spatters on the window molding on the right side of the window came from a direction similar from left to right and these on the left side of the window came from right side traveling left. So it appears that the blood came from an area below about the middle of the right-hand window.

It was noted that there were spatters on the mopboard just to the right of the window. Also there were spatters on the east wall. These were going up the wall and these again were small spatters. They were smaller than if you held your finger out and one drop fell. They were probably a tenth that size. Little bit larger than the size of a head of a pin. So that was noted. He thought there were probably about ten spatters going up the wall on the east side. Some of these spatters were behind the boxes indicating that some of the clothing had been piled on those cushions in the corner after the blood had gotten there. There were spatters traveling up the wall in an area between the dresser and the wall. There were again, these small spatters. There were some spatters noted in the corner.

At the time when he first processed the room, the dresser was in place. Later they looked when the dresser had been removed and there were apparent watermarks. If you wipe something with a sponge and some water runs from the sponge. You could see little watermarks that had run behind the dresser. They tested these and they indicated that the water marks were also mixed with blood. Indicating that this wall had been wiped and washed. Watermarks mixed with blood.

On each of the walls or at least on what would be the east and south and some of the north wall, he noted that there were tiny red fibers, adhering to the walls. These fibers had apparently came off due to roughness of the wall when the wall had been wiped or washed at some time. They checked the ceiling also and there were two spatters above the bed toward the end of the bed, but closer to the wall. Probably about two or three feet from the wall, two small spatters on the ceiling. Checking the floor. One area of scraping was the east of the end of the mattress, directly below the window. Below the right window and the other area of scraping was sort of in the middle of the room. Out from the end of the mattress, between the dresser and the mattress.

He took all the samples of Sandi's bedroom and then went down to the basement. He looked at the stains that were down in the basement. A dugout area with a concrete ledge around the outside. The area directly below the scraping on the floor, which were noted between the dresser and mattress. A scraped area that was out about in the middle of the room. In the basement there was a ledge directly underneath this area. You could see where blood had run down through the boards of the floor, and had run down onto this ledge and run off the ledge and down into the dirt floor.

There were fruit jars on the ledge, and these became spattered with blood as did some boxes on the floor. The scrape marks on the ledge are areas where he removed the blood for testing. On the ceiling area blood had run down between the cracks. Some of the blood had come down behind this two-by-four that he could not get to. There was sort of a wooden box protruding out. He did not know what the function of the box was, but the blood had run down onto the top of the box. And there was a puddle of blood inside the box where it had collected.

They then went to the kitchen area. They discovered in one drawer, two hammers, a paint scraper, and other miscellaneous tools. These were checked for the presence of blood. He removed the head of the hammer by sawing the hammer handle and forcing the remaining portion out through the top of the head of the hammer. The purpose of this was to see if there was any blood that had run down inside the hammer handle. At the scene it was noted that there was light staining on the wooden portion of the handle of the hammer. There was apparent blood crust in the claw area. On the wooden portion there were some nails and things driven into it to hold the handle in and light staining on the neck of the hammer. The hammer was placed in a bag and taken back to the lab for blood tests.

Chapter 12

LUKE 9:48

"Anyone who takes care of a little child like this is caring for me! And whoever cares for me is caring for God who sent me. Your care for others is the measure of your greatness."

HE WENT INTO THE OTHER BEDROOM THAT WAS SAID TO BE Tammy's and also shared by Harvey Hallen Jr. This area was completely processed to check for the presence of bloodstains or any other type of evidence that might be present. He then processed the entire room. He also processed a pickup truck owned by Harley Hallen Jr. The first time Terry Labber saw this truck was at the apartment on the eighth of December, the same day he had arrived at the home. He made a request that he would be allowed to look in the back of the truck for the presence of bloodstains. The back of the truck was opened and it was noted, there were two doors which swung open. It was discovered there was bloodstaining on each of the two outside doors entering into the back of the truck.

The search warrant was acquired to then search the inside of the truck on the ninth of December. The truck was placed in the fire hall in Alexandria. He began the process and found that there was bloodstaining on the left door. On the inside on the right door. That there was bloodstaining on the raised portion on the bed, where the wheel well is. On the inside of the bed there was a large area of bloodstaining or blood crusts in the center of the bed of the truck, toward the rear of the truck. Also there was bloodstaining on the beams and frame of the truck.

After the truck had sat at the firehall, he wanted to point out that on the eighth, a lot of the stains or some of the stains were removed from inside the truck bed, then the next morning he went back to finish processing the truck. He noted that apparent blood had run down on the floor underneath the truck and up towards the front of the truck, which would be the area between the cab and the box. He saw it dripping. Labber went underneath the truck to see if he could determine where the blood had originated. He noted that on the lengthwise beams and some of the cross-framing up on top of these beams there was sort of dried pools of blood. These areas of blood were scraped onto sheets of paper, which were taken back to the lab for analysis.

Chapter 13

ESTHER 2:23

An investigation was made, the two men found guilty, and impaled alive. This was all duly recorded in the book of the history of "King Ahauerus" reign.

To analyze blood to determine whether it is A, B, or AB or O is a process of taking the blood and reacting it with what is called an anti-sera. What the anti-sera is, simply put, if you have a person and you test his blood with anti A substance, which we get commercially and observe the reaction of the blood with the anti-sera, you will notice a clumping of the blood cells. This tells us that we have A type blood. It is a reaction between a prepared anti-sera and the blood that we observe microscopically. The blood in question is brought into contact with what is called anti-human material, anti-human sera, which is prepared again commercially, we observe a reaction between the bloodstain in question and this anti-human, if there is a reaction then we know this is human blood.

If it is not human, there will be no reaction. The only area of all the stains or areas in the apartment where he mentioned that he had found and noted blood, there was one small stain on a bed, OA, this would be a bed cover or bedspread, which would be Tammy's room. There was a small blood spot and he could not determine if that was of human origin. It did not react with anti-

LISA L COLSEN

human material indicating that it was not of human origin. But all the other blood found in the house reacted as being human blood. The blood found in Harley Hallen's truck was also found to be human as was the blood found on the hammer. He then began determining the blood group breakdowns of each of the stains.

He also had the opportunity to analyze a sample of blood purporting to be from Harley Hallen Jr. Harley Hallen Jr. is in a blood group type O. He is an RH, little R, which is one of the designations of the RH system, EAP type BA and PGM type one.

He also analyzed the blood of Tammy, and she was a type O, and the PGM group was type two. We had an affidavit that was submitted by Jeff McDonald, who had a license to practice medicine in the state of Minnesota. He had reviewed the blood donor records on file with the St. Paul Regional Blood Center and determined that a person who presented herself to be Sandi, gave blood in Alexandria, Minnesota on September sixteenth, 1976. That unit of blood was analyzed by technicians under the supervision and control of your affiant and was found to be of a type A positive.

Terry Labber talked to Dr. McDonald with the purpose of determining whether or not he had further broken the RH factors more than just positive or negative? He said that Sandi's blood was drawn, that they were looking for specific RH groups and that he had broken Sandi's blood down into the specific RH group as much as they do. They had tested for four of the five different antigens that we test for. Their findings were that, the most likely group that she has is the R2, little R, which is approximately three percent of the population. All the percentages which they use in their data. What they do is make a record of every single little blood that comes into the lab. They record all the different blood breakdowns. So they have a statistical data bank of what would be mainly general population of Minnesota. Now they have also correlated this with War Memorial Blood Bank in Minneapolis. They have done statistical studies on the different groupings of different individuals in Minnesota. These are again correlated with published data, which is on a national basis.

From the unit of blood that was acquired from Sandi, our findings were that three out of every one hundred people would have this particular blood type. We broke it down to three percent of this particular RH group. Because the blood bank did not do one of the antigens. Three percent of the population have four antigens, which the blood bank had determined. Three percent of the antigens, one additional, which we did. In doing RH breaking down and the sample from a dried stain, takes a considerable quantity of blood. You cannot determine the RH group, for example, from a splatter on the wall. It simply is not enough blood. In areas where there was a large concentration of blood, like in the basement and in areas of the truck, where there were large quantities of blood, there were sufficient amounts of blood to do RH grouping. Labber did do the Rh-ing, broken down in four different blood group systems in certain areas of the house and truck. In other areas he simply did not have enough blood to do RH.

In these areas he had the blood broken down as far as he could with the amount of the sample. In the basement where there were sufficient amounts. He determined the ABO blood group type as being type A. The RH group as type R2, little R. The PGM enzyme group as type one and the EAP group as type A. Three people out of every thousand people at random have this combination of blood factors. There was a spot of blood in the center of the truck bed and on this area of bloodstaining we were able to do all four of the blood grouping factors. These came out the same as the blood factors in the basement of the house. So the blood in the truck also only three people in a thousand had this combination of blood factors; it was the same as what was found in the basement.

There were actually two areas from the truck that he tested. The area in the middle of the truck bed, which is inside an area on the beams, cross-beams between the truck bed and cab where blood had apparently run down on top of these beams. This blood was collected. He was able to do all four systems of blood on these beams. This blood again was broken down from only three out of every thousand people. It was the same combination of blood factors as was found in the basement. The blood which had run onto the floor under the truck, he determined three of the groupings. He determined the two enzyme groups and AB group. Not enough blood there to do an RH grouping. He determined that, that also, was of the same three groups as the blood from the basement.

The area in the truck that he did blood grouping on was the left side, rear door. So he opened the door to go into the truck, the left-hand door. Also on the doorframe there was blood. This was consistent with the blood in the basement. There was blood on what would be the wheel well of the truck on the inside. This was also consistent with blood from the basement.

The truck Harley Hallen used to transport Sandi out of her apartment to his brother Dave Hallen's farm.

There was more than one beam underneath the truck. One beam he was able to break down all the way. The other crossbeam where there was blood, he was able to break it down into three systems. This was the same as that coming from the basement. All of the blood that he found in the house that is on the doors and on the walls was consistent with the blood in the basement. As much as he could break down the blood sample, it was consistent to what was in the basement. The hammer he was able to break that down into two systems. The blood on the hammer was type A. He was able to do one of the enzymes as found in the blood in the basement. In addition to looking for bloodstains, he also noted that there was yellow paint on the hammer. Visually it appeared to be the same color of paint that was on the walls in Sandi's bedroom.

Also, he had a can of paint that was found in the entranceway to the basement. There was paint on the handle and also a larger piece of paint on the head of the hammer. He noted that when he lifted the paint, it was not adhering very well to the hammer. He noted there were very small amounts of blood on the outside of the yellow paint, but when lifting the paint up and removing some of it for comparison, it was noted that there was blood underneath the paint as well. The fact that he found blood on the surface or outer surface of the paint and only a very small quantity, it appeared that the blood had run underneath the paint after the paint had gotten on the surface because there was very little blood around the paint sample, as if the blood had been removed from the area around the paint chip. But the blood underneath this chip had been retained there. It indicated that the paint was there at the time the blood was deposited.

The pillowcase was examined, there were several small spots of blood and these were analyzed as to their ABO type. It was type A which was similar to the blood in the basement. There was one smaller or little bit larger smear and he was able to do one enzyme grouping and this was also consistent with the blood in the basement. The flesh with hair coming from it was analyzed the same manner as a bloodstain. Blood was removed from the flesh, a small portion of the flesh was examined as if it were a bloodstain, on this piece of apparent flesh. He was able to determine the ABO blood group and the enzyme groups present in this apparent flesh. These were all of the same type as the blood found in the basement, indicating that this particular piece of apparent flesh had come from the same person as the blood in the basement.

The hairs that were coming from the piece of flesh were removed and were mounted on slides, so I could observe the hairs under a microscope. These hairs were compared to hair samples which were submitted, in compliance to articles of hair at the scene which belonged to Sandi. These samples were submitted by authorities from Alexandria. One of the hairs was from Sandi's purse and the other hairs were from a scarf. The microscopic examination showed that the hairs from the scarf, the one hair from the purse and the hairs which were attached to the piece of flesh all showed similar microscopic characteristics indicating that they came from the same person. They cannot like fingerprints say they actually did. By microscopic characteristics of the hair, noting the structure of the hair, it's coarseness, the ends of the hair. He could determine that these are head hairs opposed to hairs from other parts of the body.

He went through the entire bedroom and located the positions of all the bloodstains on the walls and ceiling. When he felt that he had found all the stains he circled the stains and then attempted to determine if these bloodstains originated from a common source or if there was more than one source and where in the room these particular stains originated from. He wanted to attempt to determine how many blows were struck, if possible. By the location of the different bloodstains. The blood spatters indicated that there was more than one blow for the simple fact that there were blood spatters and quantity of blood spatters indicated there was more than one blow. In any case of blow situations.

The size of the blood spatters first of all tells you whether or how the blood got there, so to speak. The size of the spatter, if you have whole drops of blood indicates that this blood is coming from a person of larger size, it is not characteristic of blood which is spattered off. Blood that is spattered is generally very much smaller. So the size indicated that he was actually looking at spatters of blood. The blood showed some source of origin. Blood on the right-hand side of the window was pointing towards the right and the blood on the left-hand side of the window towards the right indicated that these came from a common source, which would be consistent with a blow having been administered. The blood on the left-hand side of the window towards the right, so indicated that these came from a common source which would be consistent with a blow having been administered. When you have blows being struck, there is very little, if any bloodshed in the form of a spatter with the first blow. In order for there to be spattering there has to be blood which is being hit to cause spatter. So the spatter occurs with additional blows, in this situation there was more than one blow.

They also tested a field jacket worn by Harley Hallen Jr. On the inside lining of the jacket he noted small blood spatters. They found these to of human origin. But the amount was too small to be typed. Ladder had been on a good many homicide cases. He said, this is a considerable amount of blood. The amount of blood is more than I have found in a lot of other cases. It has been his experience that this quantity of blood is more than a simple cut or something. It seems to be massive bleeding which would be the result of a very serious wound. Blood is a liquid, when it flows from the body a reaction occurs which allows the blood or causes the blood to form a clot. That is it forms a semisolid type of material which than causes the blood to cease flowing. This is the bases of why we do not bleed to death, because the blood clots. When blood flows from a body into a pool it will clot and this will disallow it to flow.

In the basement on the ledge, there was considerable quantities of blood. The areas where he scraped the blood was fairly thick, probably around sixteenth of an inch. Very thick in different areas. This blood had to have gotten there before it coagulated. There was blood between the floor, the two floors, the main floor and the sub- floor in addition to the area of bloodstaining, which was below one of the scraped areas. There was another area which there was not a basement under. The area of scraping near the windows, blood had also run through the boards in this area and there was some cement underneath there. Again there was another pool of blood underneath this area of the floor. So this indicated that there was massive bleeding. The amount of blood that he actually observed was the blood which had run through the floor, it did not represent the blood which had apparently been scraped up from the floor. The blood to have run through there had to have been a sizable quantity, also on top of the boards.

The kitchen drawer where they located the murder weapon a common household hammer. Which she had used earlier in the day in her bedroom.

The basement where Sandi's blood led detectives to believe. Something bad had happened to her.

Chapter 14

JOHN 8:12

"I am the Light of the world. So if you follow me, you won't be stumbling through the darkness, for living light will flood your path."

ON JANUARY 24, DR. HAVEN, THE MEDICAL EXAMINER WENT TO Sandi's apartment to look at the quantities of blood there, since as of yet there was no body. He was educated at the University of Tehren. He did his internship in Tennessee and then four years of specializing in Pathology. He was the Deputy Medical Examiner. He had been a pathologist for twelve years. Dr. Haven had heard some testimony relative to quantities of blood that were found at the apartment. He said, the most important function of the blood is really just to carry oxygen for the cells as a nutrient. Not only nutrition is important, oxygen which the blood would carry, if you cut the blood circulation within an organ, within minutes that particular organ is going to die because of a lack of oxygen. That is the main significance of blood, carrying oxygen.

You can very easily identify human blood. There are many ways they can decide how much blood a person has. It goes by weight and height of a person. There are a lot of ways of figuring it out. They use isotopes. An atomic energy sort of device. We have a table. The most classic book used all over the world as authoritative figures. They show the weight of an individual and the height for men and women, so they predict how much a person would have. The text is known all over the world called, "Blood Transfusion In Clinical Medicine," by Dr. Mollison, who is a great author in England. His book is used all over the world. So it is a most classic book in blood.

Knowing the weight and height of an individual one can estimate closely what would be the blood volume. If you have a female and she is approximately sixty-six inches tall and weighs approximately one hundred and thirty pounds. Which would be five feet, six inches tall, an individual is estimated at about 3,815 cc. That would be between seven or eight pints of blood. Most people understand pints, but scientifically, talking about 3,815 cc's. He did see some of the blood at the apartment. The day He was there they were digging the floor. He had a chance to see how much blood had seeped in the floor. When he got there to inspect the floor, it was cleaned. He did not get a chance to see how much blood was on the floor, but he had seen how much blood seeped through the floor. The blood on the wall in the basement had been washed already. But, he looked at photographs. The amount of blood that there was on the wall, ceiling, beneath the boards and then what he could see on the photo's that had gone through the floor down into the basement, which was already erased when he got there.

When blood is shed, it does not matter who and under what circumstances blood coagulates, it really does not run. How much of it had been wiped? He could not tell. What he could tell, it was significant amounts of blood, what he felt was massive bleeding. To him anything over twenty percent he considered massive bleeding. A person can lose twenty percent of their blood, they start getting shocky, till they get medical attention right away. If they do not get medical attention, they will continue bleeding. It would be unlikely someone with that kind of bleeding, with no medical attention would survive. Finding a piece of scalp would indicate to me that a blow to the head had been sustained. Any person with a head injury, that massive bleeding, in itself could be fatal. But, most of the people with head injuries either get a skull fracture or brain injury too. All head injuries due to any cause, automobile accident, trauma, or homicide, or any. When they get brain injury or get head injury, they usually associate with a skull fracture and brain injury too. That would make the person even less likely to survive. Head or scalp wounds generally bleed more because of tautness, the lack of elasticity, arteries do not contract.

Some areas if we bleed or cut them, the tissue contracts and bleeding is stopped. Some areas like the scalp just do not contract. They bleed more.

Once a person dies, the blood coagulates but, in certain circumstances, particularly in a head injury. A person can still bleed after death. If there was communication with sinuses, they can. That means if there is a trauma enough to cause a skull fracture and communication of the wound, certain fractures in the brain called sinuses that can cause bleeding. So head injuries unusual in that, they can still bleed after death.

Chapter 15

HEBREWS 11:13

These men of faith I have mentioned died without ever receiving all that God had promised them.

A S THE GRAND JURY WAS HEARING THE EVIDENCE IN THIS MATTER, the police force was hard at work trying to locate Sandi's body. The police had searched several areas resulting from tips phoned into the department. One of them a long-distance caller directed them to a wooded area overlooking Crestwood Hills, across the road and up a hill from the Crestwood Ski Hill. A team of some eighteen city police, county sheriff, and law enforcement students from the Alexandria Tech School spent several hours combing the area on the fourteenth, without success. Chief George McKay says his department, with the help of the SCB and the County Sheriff's department will be staying on top of any and all leads that come into the department.

"We are working on this almost around the clock," he said. He also added that authorities are stymied from moving too fast in other areas of the case until Sandi is found. Chief McKay said, "Tips in the case are coming in from many sources, some good and some bad, but we have to consider each and every one of them. We have had some rather eerie calls pertaining to this case. Let's just say we have checked, hoping for the best. She is out there somewhere!" Douglas County Sheriff's posse members were dispatched to Union Lake, South of Alexandria, the twenty-third. They searched a wooded area near the lake and used shovels to uncover a soft dirt pile in a road ditch nearby. Posse members also looked through several vacant farm buildings in the area, but found nothing. Volunteer search crews combed many parts of the country and countless property owners have searched their own land in hopes of finding where the possible murder victim could have been dumped or buried. "She could be any place," said one member. "Even two hundred miles away, who knows?"

A large section of Carlos State Park was checked out by an organized search on the thirtieth and thirty-first without success. Through the efforts of the KSTP News in Minnesota, newsman Jason Doris, at the stations expense, flew Chicago psychic Gary Warren to Alexandria. Using a photo of Sandi. He attempted to "reach" her by holding in his hands a blouse and necklace she owned. Warren rattled off a number of would-be clues. To no avail. Police spent several hours searching vacant farm buildings, two to three miles North of ABW Inc. They also had a woman call them who wanted to remain anonymous although she is from the state of Illinois, she described to police what she "saw" happen inside the apartment. She also suggested a possible route out of town the suspected killer took, using landmarks along the way. That route also ended Northeast of the city, about a mile or two West from where Gary Warren "sees her."

In a nutshell, the woman, described in considerable detail, what she visioned happening inside the apartment the night Sandi disappeared, the route the vehicle, with Sandi inside, allegedly took out of town, and approximately where the victims shallow burial site could be found! Chief George McKay, slightly less apprehensive since listening to what at least appeared to be rather vivid description of Alexandria area landmarks by someone who had never set eyes upon the area, he decided to check it out. Some of the places the woman described rang very true years after Sandi was found. But, at the time it led the search to Noonan Park, (wire fence), past the Eagles Lodge, (flashing lights), over the Carlos-Le-Homme- Dieu Bridge, a right turn down a country road twenty along the North side of Lake Le Homme Dieu. The road emptied onto a section of road made unusually rough because of a sewer construction project, then down the tree-ladened Northeast drive in front of Kruger's farm.

The woman directed authorities to an area she described as a popular place for young kids to hold outdoor parties, (which now I know would be Inspiration Peak). She said the victim was buried in a shallow grave within eyesight of a lake, (which never came of anything). She said, "If I were a giant, I could take one big step and be at the scene of your 1974 murder." Chief McKay confirmed that Rosaleen Petersen was found dying only about one-half mile North of the scene described by the clairvoyant woman. Mrs. Petersen had been brutally beaten and died several days after being found lying on a little used Carlos township road early one February morning. That case has not been solved. The posse spent several days searching for the "shallow grave" with no success. "Whether you believe in psychic powers or not," George McKay said, "this woman told us somethings about the case we know are true and her description of the overall scene at the apartment, the possible route the assailant took out of town, description of landmarks and so on was too coincidental to avoid.

Local Law Enforcement along with Sandi's family are offering a thousand-dollar reward for any information leading to the recovery and conviction of her assailant. And for people to search their property, culverts, vacant buildings, abandoned vehicles, wooded areas, "any place where she could possibly have been hidden," said George McKay. Authorities do have a suspect in the case and are presently considering making an arrest, even if Sandi's body is not found. Attorney Rolf said that to prove to a jury "beyond a reasonable doubt," there was a murder without having found the body is always difficult." "However." he added, "it might be a risk we have to take."

A man from Parkers Prairie, Minnesota was taken into custody January fourth. Police identified the man as Harley Art Hallen Jr. An unemployed bachelor who shared an Alexandria apartment with Tammy Lewin, his former friend, and Sandi. Hallen will be arranged January sixth, and charged with two counts, one first degree murder, count two, first degree murder with sexual intent and second-degree murder and kidnapping, according to the complaint initiated by Chief George McKay. Authorities had listed Hallen as a suspect for some time in what County Attorney Rolf and other law enforcement officials believe to be more than just a case of a missing girl. Hallen was arrested at 5:00 P.M. by authorities who stopped him while he was driving his truck in Parkers Prairie. Since Sandi's disappearance began, he has been living with his parents in Parkers Prairie Trailer court, owned by his father. The family only moved to the community two or three years ago. He offered no resistance.

Both counts carry a maximum penalty upon conviction of life, if convicted by a jury of first-degree murder, if convicted of second degree murder the sentence is three to forty years. The kidnapping charge adds 40,000 dollars or both. Authorities moved on the case and made the arrest based on what county attorney Rolf explained as sufficient probable cause, including human blood in both the apartment and the suspect's vehicle.

Authorities are certain Sandi is not alive, and that she was attacked in her apartment and her body transported out of the city, somewhere and hidden. Shortly before eleven Am, Hallen was handcuffed and escorted from the jail to the court house by Chief George McKay, seated with three defense attorneys. Hallen answered, "Yes, sir" when Judge Baland asked if he understood his rights, and the nature of the complaint against him. Much of the discussion centered around the amount of bail to be set. Hallen's attorneys, pleaded with the judge to keep the amount of bail low enough so that Hallen could be at liberty between court appearances. County Attorney Rolf told the court "We are dealing with a serious crime, one that we believe to be a very violent act! We have quite a bit of evidence to lead one to believe that the defendant committed this crime. We are asking you, Judge, to take into consideration that bond be set at $100,000. Hallen's attorney said anything over $5,000 would be grossly excessive, pointing to the fact that Hallen remained in the area for nearly a month before this arrest while knowing that he was a suspect and that there was no reason to believe he would do otherwise if allowed to post bail. Judge Baland granted the State's request and set bail at $100,000. He set Hallen's next court date for January fourteenth at the Douglas County Court house. Hallen's attorneys said they would appeal the $100,000 bond in district court.

The grand jury was summoned on January twenty-eighth at the Douglas County court house. Although second degree murder charges have been filed against the suspect, the jury could indict him on first degree murder, if in their judgment the evidence would support such a determination. They could also determine that no indictment is warranted. The real evidence in the case, a body, has yet to be found. Hallen will make his next court appearance January fourteenth.

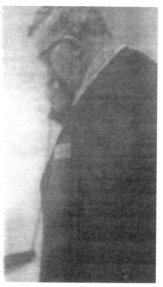

Harley Hallen Jr leaving the Alexandria Courthouse after being indicted on 1st degree murder charges.

Chief George McKay receiving the phone call that they had found Sandi's body.

The arrest of Harley Hallen Jr.

Chapter 16

PHILIPPIANS 4:6

Don't worry about anything, instead, pray about everything, tell God your needs and don't forget to thank him for his answers.

AFTER LISTENING NEARLY THREE DAYS TO THE EVIDENCE COMPILED by the law enforcement personnel, the nineteen members of the Grand Jury returned two indictments against Hallen. Murder in the first degree and murder in the second degree. They deliberated three hours before announcing their decision. Although, invited to appeal and be questioned before the jury, Hallen declined. Hallen's attorney entered a plea of innocent to both counts. Hallen's attorney's requested that the trial be moved out of Douglas County. They were granted a change of venue. The trial was set to begin Monday, April 18 at Morrison County Courthouse in Little Falls, Minnesota.

Hallen's attorneys had written to Judge Sater, indicating that Hallen was willing to waive a jury trial if Hallen's case was heard by a judge without a jury, then it was possible that it would be held at the court house in Alexandria rather than Little Falls and sooner than April 18. By waving the right to a jury, it would the defense was optimistic that Hallen would fare better by pleading the case before the judge. It was believed that Hallen's attorney would be asking that the charges be dropped, because there was no direct proof, that a crime had even been committed.

There are case histories where people have been convicted of crimes without finding a body. However, there is no such precedent in Minnesota, which is one of a few states that have the "direct proof," statutes on the books. The Minnesota Law dates back to before the turn of the century. In the meantime, the pace has been picked up and the search was now centered on the body of water behind the Burlington-Northern Railroad Depot. Acting on a tip, authorities had scuba divers plunging through holes in the ice late last week. However the waters were too dark and efforts had to be curtailed. Search crews are scheduled to head for several wooded areas, and as soon as the skies cleared, airplanes will be used. Now that the snow cover had gone, local authorities are hopeful that if Sandi has been disposed of in some manner, she can be found. Activity in her search has been accelerated because of the pending trial of Hallen. Set to begin April 18. Those plans have now been scrapped as Hallen has since waived his right to a jury trial.

Authorities are scouring the area in hopes of finding Sandi before the case goes to court. On March 31, 1977, the body of my sister Sandi was found. "We have all been in the police business for over twenty years," George McKay said last week after news that the body of Sandi had been found. "We had been looking where everyone else was telling us to look and we finally decided to revert back to the basic, nuts-and-bolts police work." The pressure to find Sandi was mounting rapidly with the trial starting. McKay and several other law enforcement officers from the city, county, and state got together early last week to review the whole matter. Based on what McKay called, "basic police work," it was determined that a certain wooded area about one and a half miles from Urbank, Minnesota should be searched again. The area had been covered in a routine search last winter but nothing was found.

Authorities had reason to believe that she was, "in those woods somewhere!" A search warrant was obtained and the six men were combing the woods at his brothers farm. Ottertail Deputy Melfry, noticed a pile of brush in the woods and wondered out loud whether or not it was attached to the ground. It was not. After clearing the limbs and other debris away, Melfry stepped on the part of the ground that had been covered and he quickly saw that it was soft and that the dirt had recently been disturbed. Sandi's body was taken to Fergus Falls, Minnesota. Where an autopsy would determine the exact cause of death.

Hallen now changed his mind and said he would like a jury trial. His attorneys said that they would be ready for trial by the eighteenth of April. The turnabout by the defense was the result of new evidence in the case, that being the discovery of Sandi's body. Hallen's attorney's would be investigating the possibility of pleading mental illness on behalf of Hallen. Hallen and his attorneys now excepted a plea bargain. They dropped the first-degree murder and count three first-degree to second-degree murder. The court action which involved no jury, ends a case, which came to light four months after the death of Sandi. Hallen took the stand and testified that he had been drinking, but was not drunk. He had been to the drinking establishment called "The Barn." He said he stayed at "The Barn" till about eleven or twelve midnight.

When he got home, Sandi was there sleeping in her bedroom. He went in there and engaged in conversation with her. They argued and she told him she would have him moved out of the apartment. He then picked up a hammer that was on a box in her bedroom just a little ways from her bed, and struck her several times in the head. When he picked up the hammer he intended to kill her. He then removed her from her home and put her in his truck. Took her to his brother's farm. He then put her in the swamp, or woods and returned back to Alexandria to the apartment to clean up the blood and other evidence. The next day he returned to his brother's and rode his three-wheeler by her body for no particular reason. He just drove by. Six days later he returned to his brother's farm and took a shovel from there and buried her.

County Attorney Rolf said, he had no evidence to substantiate first-degree murder, which he said was very difficult to prove under the present court system. Establishing premeditation before a jury, he said, is quite rare and added, first-degree murder convictions are few and far between. Hallen showed little or no emotion as he smiled as they led him back to jail. He would be later transferred to Stillwater State Prison. Sandi was found March 31, Mom's birthday. The next day was April 1. Chief George McKay's birthday, he said it was the best present he ever received. The television cameras were there to record the pain in her family's eyes and let this tragedy sink into each viewer's mind. To remind people that, yes, these things do happen in the small American town.

We buried our sister that day, the sounds of our mom's cries echoing off the hills and left our tears to mingle on the cold ground. Reluctant to leave her once again alone in the cold ground. Mom returned in the night to sit by her grave. Sandi was not there anymore. I know she made her journey to heaven the night she was murdered, to be with Jesus, the one who loved her most and deepest.

Chapter 17

HEBREWS 6:18

He has given us both his promise and his oath, two things we can count on, for it is impossible for God to tell a lie.

WE HAD SANDI'S FUNERAL ON APRIL 4. A VERY SAD DAY. OUR hopes were over. We have our buried treasure now. She was laid to rest in a little Finnish Church Cemetery. Where seventeen years later my mom would be buried beside her. I have my own ideas about that day. Harley Hallen took my sister's life. Of course, it is speculation, but sometimes you can read the blood trail. The only one who knows for sure is Harley Hallen himself. Someday it would have been nice to see the man face-to-face.

On the night my sister was to be picked up by our mom. She for whatever reason did not make it there to get her. Harley Hallen stated that Tammy left at eight o'clock to go on her date and that Sandi was laying on the couch reading a book. The neighbors upstairs said that the stereo went real loud at around eight thirty or there about. The neighbors stated they heard thumping against the wall. In previous testimony. Hallen stopped at the Knute Nelson Memorial Home, strangely Sandi's workplace. He made a call to a garage at eight fifteen. He told them that his truck would not start. The gentleman came there, was going to give him a jump. Hallen said it did not need a jump. The gentleman got inside and pumped it a couple times and it started.

Hallen asked what he owed him, he said, "Four dollars."

Hallen stated, "How come so much? You didn't do anything!" He said that was what he was supposed to charge. He then paid him and took off across the lawn. The gentleman said he acted very strange and nervous. I believe he was using the use of the phone and the gentleman as an alibi. I believe right after or soon after Tammy left. Harley Hallen, raped and killed my sister. I believe he forced himself upon her and she ran from that couch and he went after her! After his vicious rape of her, she threatened him with calling the police. He did not want that to happen. He picked up the hammer, where she had laid it from hanging pictures earlier in the day, struck her at least three times. I believe that she fought off these attacks with this hammer he used on her. I have drawn out the setup of the apartment and all that the testimony from the crime lab stated, where they found blood. Very little blood was found in any of the rooms. Such as the kitchen, Tammy's bedroom, some leading outside by the door. A few by the arm of the couch. Some in what we called the entryway. All other blood was found in her bedroom. These pinpoint to the fact that her life possibly was taken there.

There were three sites, where massive amounts of blood were found. Number one, the mattress, number two, the scraped marks on the floor facing the door, and number three, the other side of the bed on the floor underneath the window. I believe these three sites is where her body lay at different times. There was no blood trail leading from her bedroom through the living room. So I believed he wrapped her in the bed sheets that were missing off her bed, put her in the back of his truck, made the one stop at the nursing home for an alibi plus used the mechanic for one, so someone saw him at eight fifteen to eight thirty. He then took her out to his brother's farm. Dropped her body off alongside a swamp. Where one of the sheriffs told me she lay for six days, the children on the farm could have seen her body if they would have been looking.

He then returned to the apartment and tried to clean up the blood and stuff before Tammy returned. Then I believe he went to the "Barn." Witnesses testify to the fact that they saw Hallen at about ten thirty that night. He then went to his brother's the next day. Took his three-wheeler and drove by Sandi's body. Than left and six days after he took my sister's life, he returned and dug a shallow grave and buried her body. Hoping that she would never be found.

Deputies stated to me that my sister was nude when she was found. I ponder all this as I write and I feel my sister's terror as she must have tried to protect herself. (I hear my echoes, *"Grab the hammer, Sandi! Hurry!"* But she was no killer. Running from someone she did not know. I feel her heart pounding from the fear of being attacked and raped. Of trying to escape! I run with her away, to search for a safe place to hide! Here alongside the bed! Hurry! To rid herself of the unimaginable violence. I feel the instant seconds of pain as her attacker grabbed her the very first time. How he carried her body out to his truck. Was she still alive? Blood in the truck was massive. Did she know what was being done? I like to say no. He drove to his brother's farm and threw her out along a swamp. Not covering her body. But just leaving her alone and naked to lay atop the hard cold unforgiving earth. To drive by the next day "just because," is what he stated, "no reason!" To leave her laying out there exposed for six days!

This is the sadness of our Sandi's death. Harley Hallen (I am not sure why I am protecting his identity), treated Sandi as though she were nothing. As he stated in his testimony, when asked where he had put Sandi, he said, "I put it in the swamp or woods, first being the edge of the swamp and six days later, burying it in the woods farther in. He never thought of her as a human being. He just used her as an object. After forty-five years the thoughts of what he did to her are as vivid as 1976. I know what must have happened. I have read every piece of paper and spoken to almost every officer that was involved in her case.

My many years of questions that did not make sense to me have been answered. Was it a fair sentence that Harley Hallen Jr. received that day in April. For himself, yes I am sure he thought so. For Sandi, "No!" That is what the county attorney plea-bargained. So he served six and a half years for raping and killing my sister. He was twenty-five years old when he went to prison and came out at thirty-one. And I deal with that. Do I accept it? I have to. I struggle with the why of it all. Not only did Harley Hallen murder and take away a person that we loved dearly, but he left this family with so many scars. So in truth it is a death sentence for all of us. The struggles we have in trying to heal ourselves, forty-five years later.

Chapter 19

LAMENTATIONS 3:37

Matters not who says a thing will or won't happen unless the Lord determines that it should.

OH, YES I COULD BANG MY HEAD AGAINST A HARD WALL AND SAY, it was not fair! Say he should have spent his life behind bars, that he should have rotted off the planet of this earth! I answer myself, he was in front of one judge. But he has not stood in front of the final! If Jesus has the compassion to forgive a murderer, am I so much greater than our Savior, to be able to not forgive. I can hate everything about the murderer and the terror he caused our family and our beloved Sandi. I can hate everything about that and still forgive the person for those actions. I know Sandi would not have wanted us to carry hate and feel vengeful. She would have wanted me to be thankful! God, let her grace us, with her presence for the seventeen years we had with her. I will not sit here and say it has been easy.

It has been a forty-five-year journey, and some roads were pure hell! Sandi is no longer of this world, but her family is! I had to shake myself from the dreams that she would return. Harley Hallen Jr. was released from prison in 1981. Sandi would have been twenty-three years old. I think back to how my sister had died, she was hit with a claw hammer, not once but several times. As her attacker faced her! She was wrapped in her bed sheets with nothing on to cover her, thrown in the back of his truck, hauled away to a farm, dumped onto the edge of a swamp and was hidden from her loved ones. They were looking in every place they could possibly think of, just wishing anyone would find her. As he made at least several trips back out to her to make sure he kept his secret hidden in the cold.

I wondered if all that, in what he had done to her and her family was worth the six and a half years they took from his life? He was still alive. Today 2021, he lives in Mound, Minnesota, is married, owns a business, has children. So when I was twenty-two, I decided I couldn't rely on our justice system to be fair to anyone who was a victim. I felt they were placing values on human lives. If you had a name or title of importance and were harmed or murdered you would be doing what they call, "Hard Time," if you ever saw daylight again! But if you were common folk, you were just another victim, no life sentence, no television coverage. The sentences were not as stiff. Fairness in the legal system only occurred if you had a title to that name. Football, Basketball, Actor, Actress, Governor, etc.

So this began the healing of me, in 1977 after Sandi was in her sleeping spot and life was supposed to be okay, it never really recovered from Hallen's actions. Mom slid so far down the hill of alcoholism after Sandi's death. It was like there was nothing she cared about anymore, her reasons for life were done, the one person who had some control in her drinking behavior was gone now. When Harley Hallen took Sandi's life, it seemed he also killed a part of my mom also. Mom and Ray spent a lot of time drinking and fighting with each other. Alcoholism was a deep pit that we lived in. We each dealt with it in different ways. Some stayed away from our house so they didn't have to deal with Mom and her hurtful wrath. I stayed and became a mother to Mom. I became the person who made sure cigarettes were put out.

I lived my life to try to keep her happy. To agree with everything she said, although she didn't say a lot. She was a lost soul, so much had happened to her, she did not know where to begin to heal, or even how to go about starting to heal. I even began to believe, she would not be able to survive without me there to keep her going. She had lost one daughter, that she stood next to and looked up to with such love. I vowed that I would surpass everything in my life to keep anyone from hurting her ever again. So, began my journey down a long and sick road with her. To keep her from feeling hurt and lost. I truly loved my mom, more than maybe even myself.

I was so scared to go to sleep at night for fear that I would find something I did not want to the next morning. I was afraid to let her go to town at night, was afraid that she would never make it home without rolling the car over, but yet I was afraid to ride with her. Let's face it, she was drunk, she would be all over the road! I would be so scared that neither one of us would make it home. I turned those fears into myself and climbed into the car next to her because she was my mom and I swore I would never let anyone or anything happen to her. After Sandi's funeral, Mom seldom mentioned her, but I knew she was there with her. I knew Mom somehow felt that if she would have picked Sandi up that weekend, that she would have been alive. I knew that was a lot of the reason Mom spiraled down into the black hole of despair. She blamed herself as though she could have prevented this from happening.

I knew Hallen was bent on raping and killing my sister, no amount of weekends would have prevented that! Mom would never talk about it, just another trip to the bar, till she was back in a cloud. She would get agitated and strike out at you with her angry, painful words, as if she were trying to drive you away so she would not end up failing you the way she felt she had failed Sandi. I stood my ground with her in her agitated moments. She was so important in my life! I did not care whether she was drunk or sober; it did not matter to me. She was my mom. I would help her and protect her no matter what. She would be drunk and say the most mean and hurtful things, but it did not matter. I would cram the hurt and the sadness that was caused by her drunken words and I would love her even more. I knew, she really wanted me there in her heart beside her.

Chapter 20

PSALMS 3:6

And now, although ten thousand enemies surround me on every side, I am not afraid.

I MOVED AT THE AGE OF SEVENTEEN. I GOT A JOB AND MOVED TO THE same town my sister was killed in. I wondered if Mom was scared for me, being the same age as my sister when she was murdered. Mom seemed to slow down a bit on her drinking. She would come to my little apartment with rolls and sandwiches, since it was just a room and had no kitchen. I thought, *how could she take care of me! I'm supposed to take care of you!* I lived in Alexandria for almost one year. In 1979 I met a guy and all I ever wanted was someone to take care of me. I was always so shy. I would never live in an alcoholic home again. We knew each other for two weeks and got married. I wanted so desperately for someone to love me at the time not knowing him did not matter. Ray gave me away. I thought I was happy. I had not even started grieving Sandi's death.

Back when she died I gave of myself to make sure everyone else was coping and grabbing there hand to keep them from falling. I never got to see if Lisa wasn't falling. At the time it did not matter to me. I saw my brother and mom so near the edge so many times that I could not fall to pieces and have no one there in case they needed someone to lean on. I started out my married life the same scared little girl that Sandi kept telling me not to be. I was so quiet, so afraid that if I said or did something wrong, that I would be left alone with no one. So I began to drink. Just not letting myself feel. Kept saying I would never become what I lived. Instead I would become her, in every way! My husband drank a lot. He would leave home and I would not see him until days later. He would never give an explanation to where he had been. He would come home sick.

The day I went into labor, Mom was there at the hospital to hold a damp cloth to my forehead and order all the nurses around. In the wee hours of the morning, my son was born. We named him Brian Norman Ray, after his father and his two grandfathers. I looked down at him and made a promise that he would never face what I had faced as a child. I came home from the hospital and my husband left and I did not see him again for a week. When he returned, he was sick and ready to recover sleeping. I lived with him telling me to mind my business, I was a bitch, and a f —cker, and I was a dog, and they belonged on the floor in the corner. I endured, because I thought my son needed his father, because I was raised without one. And he needed to have his.

We then moved to Sebeka, Minnesota, and I did not get to see Mom much. I would bring Brian down to stay with her sometimes on the weekends. I always told myself, no matter what, my son would never face the sadness and abuse in his life that I had faced. He would grow up with parents that loved him and cared about him. And most importantly, never have to endure his parents as alcoholics. In 1981, I delivered a baby girl. My husband was nowhere around. I had not seen him in a few days. I woke up and was in labor and my brother Oscar was staying with us. He drove me and Brian to the neighbors who were going to watch him while I was at the hospital. My husband came a couple hours later. He was hungover and smelled of booze. I hated the drinking.

I gave birth to my baby girl, Amanda Mae! Named her after the sister I loved and missed so much. I wanted to so much keep my sister's memory alive. It seemed she was slipping away. No one remembered her life! She was seldom brought up in conversation. It was not fair! She needed to be remembered! She was still so close to my heart, as yet she is these many years later. One evening, thirteen days after my daughter was born, I was watching TV. It was around nine o'clock. The neighbor came over and said I had a phone call. We never had our own phone at the time. So I drove into town and used the pay phone. The call had come from my mom back home. When she answered, she was crying. Something my mom did rarely. She said Ray had died of a sudden heart attack. I started to cry, this was the only real father I had ever known, who actually wanted to be my dad! My mind drifted back to when I had first come home from foster care and had met him. I knew at that moment that this man would take care of me and be the dad I always wanted. I felt sad, and I had realized something so very important. Through Mom and my stepdad's alcoholism, there were times, that him and Mom fought, I would generally always blame him. Thinking he was the cause of Mom's unhappiness.

On August 13, we laid Ray to rest beside our sister. At the old Finnish Church Cemetery. I watched Mom again in her pain, maybe realizing some of the mistakes she had made with him. Wishing perhaps she could take things back that were said between them. Ray was a very generous man, kind and compassionate. He loved his ready-made family because he loved her. Mom just continued on in her drinking. Lonnie by now was the only one living at home. After Ray's death, we moved from Sebeka to the house Ray built for my mom. I was very happy living there! I had all the memories there. From bad to good times. It is hard to let go of memories and move on with your life. I could almost hear the laughter of us kids as we played corncob football! Or tag, "Last one to the barn is a rotten egg!" I could hear the whispers of sadness, in the quiet of the night. I wanted to keep it all, because in giving it up, I thought that Sandi would think I had forgotten her.

When we moved to Mom's house, Mom moved to Brandon, Minnesota. After Ray's death, they had to have an auction and sold everything. The house was put up for sale. Ray's construction equipment was sold. Mom and Ray had drunk themselves into debt. Mom moved in with a man I did not like. He also drank a lot and although Mom never told me when I visited her there, I believe in certain ways he was abusive to her. Mom's house was soon sold, so we moved by Garfield. I was so sad that day we moved away from the only real home that I could remember. It seemed we were leaving Ray and Sandi and forgetting they ever existed. I left our laughter and our sadness and our tears and tried to go on with my life. Mom soon left the man she was living with in Brandon. Needless to say I was very happy about that! I always thought he was very bad for her. Mom moved in with me and my husband in 1983. Now I was dealing with two alcoholics.

Mom was drinking quite regular again. I did not harp on her about quitting. I accepted her. All that mattered was that my children knew who she was and that when she was not drinking, she was the most caring mom and grandma that they would ever remember. So she would sit up late and drink in the darkness, coming in late from the bar. I started taking care of her the same as I had been doing so long ago as a teenager. Once again, making sure that no cigarettes were left burning after she passed out. Going to bed and praying to a God I hardly knew and believed did not care anyway that she would find the strength to quit drinking. I believed with all my heart I would see her sober and free of the cravings of alcohol someday.

In the later part of '83, we moved from outside of Garfield into town and Mom moved with us. My husband was drinking a lot at the time, never coming home. So, I was dealing with Mom's alcoholism and also his. One night, it was late in the evening, and my husband had been gone for several days and Mom had been up at the bar all day. They got home about the same time. They started arguing, I thought back to trying to separate her and Ray or her and my brother! When they would be fighting. I started to cry. My husband told me to kick her out and if I didn't, he was leaving and never coming back! I called the police and they came and he kept yelling at me to choose and who I was going to choose? Him or my mom! I could not! I could never ask my mom to leave my home! She needed to know that she could count on me for everything! I would even let my husband walk out that door! She had to know that I would never forsake her and act like I did not know who she was.

So the police sent my husband away. He went back to whatever dive he had been to. I felt I had no options in my decision. It seemed like I always had to hurt someone in making choices I thought were right when it came to my mom. My husband came back a couple days later. The incident was never brought up. Nobody ever faced the drinking problems. Mom remained in my home until she met Kenny Cichy, in the later part of '83. He was another alcoholic, who had lost his wife to cancer. She also drank a lot. Mom became his friend and housekeeper. They got along and were very close. He was a very nice guy. Soon after, me and my husband moved to Alexandria. Where I then became what my mom was.

Chapter 21

JEREMIAH 3:14

O sinful children, come home, for I am your master and I will bring you again to the land of Israel—one from here and two from there, wherever you are scattered.

An Alcoholic! Me! It seemed to happen overnight, when I wasn't looking! I was home alone all the time, with my son and daughter. My husband drank, he was never home. It seemed my life was quickly slipping away. What I had promised myself so many times. I was looking through the mirror at myself to only see what my mom had been. The times of drinking I can remember bits and pieces. Most of them days are a fog of strange parts still hidden from my memory. The blackouts came. I was starting to raise my children the same way we had been raised by my mom and my dad. I felt shameful. I remember thinking that when I drank, I was a whole different person. I could open up and talk to people. I was not the shy, scared little girl that I had been, as I was when I was not using. I could look at people and not feel I was never worthy. These people accepted me for what I was. I would go out at night after my husband would go to work. So he would never know. On the weekend he would leave and go drinking and not come back home till Sunday night. I always figured I could handle my drinking. I did not have a problem with it. That was my mom's problem.

One evening, a drinking friend of mine, an alcoholic, came over. It was late, my husband had gone to work. She had been drinking, and she asked me if I wanted to go have just a couple of beers. My son and daughter were both sleeping. I said sure, that they would stay sleeping and we wouldn't be gone that long. "Yes!" I knew it was wrong! My heart screamed not to leave them! But, that moment alcohol superseded the most important things to me! No, I do not recall most of the night. Alcoholics don't just have just one and leave. They stay till they are obliterated.

I awoke the next morning. It was daylight, and I was sleeping in the woods near town. I never made it back to my kids. My husband got off work that morning at seven. The kids had gotten up and Momma was not there, so my son went to the neighbors. He was about four years old. I did not return until much later. Someone at the bar put drugs in my drink. I remember nothing of what had occurred only bits and pieces. I finally went home sick, sober, and ashamed at what I had done, knowing you can never outrun the pain you have caused yourself and everyone else. Nor the pain inside you. But did this event stop me and my sickness? No! I swore to myself that I would never leave my kids alone again. To have a drink. And as much as I drank I kept that one promise. After that I always made sure that someone watched them. I would not stay out at night as much or I would take them to my sisters and they would be able to stay overnight and be with her kids. No. I was not leaving them all alone, but I was still leaving them without their mom.

I wanted so much to just drink. To forget everything, to forget who I was. To lose me in the nothingness of alcohol. But I held on to something. The anchor—if I surrender to my abuse, I would lose my kids. I would be alone. I would go out to my mom's and talk to her about her drinking and tell her to slow down, try to quit! Then in another breath, meet her at the bar and sit and get drunk with her! No, I didn't understand what I was doing. Why I was doing the things I was. Sometimes I felt I was crazy! One day I went to my mom's. It was early morning and I walked in. Mom had just gotten out of bed. I watched her walk down the hall from the bathroom to the kitchen, like I saw her do a million times before.

She headed to what I called her liquor cabinet. She was going to make herself a drink and I watched as her hands shook and I realized her disease was my disease. If I wanted to go on for years like this. I would be shaking for my next drink also. Right now I craved it! But I could still go awhile before I needed that high feeling to feel human. Seeing my mom's hands shaking and knowing I had the same illness as she, did not stop me overnight. No, I continued on in my drinking. Always being able to judge Mom in her illness and never clearly looking at my own for what it was. I always supported her in her drinking.

Us kids got together and decided we would have someone go out and talk with mom, and try to make her see what she was doing to herself. We went through a counselor in Alexandria. Surprisingly, to me that counselor was Chief George McKay's daughter. So once again the man I considered an angel on earth would enter or lives six years after our sisters murder! But in a very different way. She and two sheriffs went out to mom's. Mom told them to get off her property, that she did not want them there! She started shoving them out and they handcuffed her and put her in the back of the squad car. I was not there when they did this to her or I believe in my own sickness I would have never let them treat her like that. I would have tried to prevent it.

She was taken to detox at the hospital. The next day when she was half sober, I tried to see her and she refused to see any of us. She was kept in detox for three days. The day my mom got out of detox she called me for a ride. I was really surprised because she had been refusing to see me. She was sent to the outpatient rehab center, Hazelden Treatment Center for assessment. She was willing to go. I took her there, and they said she did not qualify for their outpatient program. She told me she was not mad because we had called someone to come and talk to her, but that they handcuffed her like a criminal she said.

I am sure that was very embarrassing for her. She returned out to Kenny's and it was six months before she had another drink. She was looking good, the trembling in her hands slowly went away. I would go over with the kids to visit her. I, of course, was still active in my drinking. But then I did not have the problem my mom had. Mine was different! Her problem was a much bigger problem than mine was!

One night of drinking I woke up in the morning in the wrong place. That day I will never in this lifetime ever feel the humiliation that I felt that early morning. I was sick, physically, more so emotionally. This was one thing that I considered to be the most impact on my quitting. I had hit my rock bottom.

I was out of control. No, I never went to my husband with the truth of what happened. I tried to live with the guilt eating me. It got to the point where I could not face him. So I left and went and stayed with my brothers. My husband would come over and ask what he had done, and I could never answer him. I could not explain and see the hurt in his eyes and I knew he would probably kill me.

Then he found out the secret I harbored, the secret I was trying to outrun. He called me every name he could think of, and I knew those to be true from all the years we had lived together. And I took another drink to calm the monster inside me! I drove to our house with a lot of prayers, to the unknown God to me, that He would give him the ability to forgive me and let me have a second chance to rebuild what I had destroyed. I walked into our house, he was sitting on the couch and we talked. I couldn't remember the situation when he asked with the other guy. I know there was a lot of drinking and smoking pot and all of a sudden it's gone. I remember being in the bar. I don't recall how I left. I do remember when I woke up, that something was very wrong and why I could not recall what went on that devastated by life!

The day I asked for a second chance, was the day I signed myself into an outpatient treatment center. I walked into that program feeling worthless and so ashamed of myself. I could not look into anyone's face because they would be able to see the ugliness of me. I learned that my disease was not because of my mom. It was not because of my husband. It was mine. I had to own it and I had to be the one to claim it! I learned that coming from a two-parent alcoholic home, I had an eighty percent chance of having some form of drinking or chemical abuse. But that I could change that, starting with myself. I did a six-week program. Me and my husband had a long road ahead of us to heal ourselves. Now I had my recovery. It did not depend on something my husband said to me. It was mine I could decide if I wanted to keep it or throw it all away. It is not the tenth drink that will give me a problems it is the first.

I had been going out to Mom's on and off. She was getting so far in her recovery. One day I decided to take the kids out to visit. They liked playing with the dogs and the chickens. I got there and no one was home. Well, I thought that they had gone into town to have a pop or something. So I went into Brandon and their vehicle was parked in front of the bar. Not a big deal to me. I went through the back door. Mom had her back to me and I remember that she turned and looked as I walked in and quickly, she grabbed the straw out of her glass. I remember how swiftly her actions were. Like a kid caught with his hand in the cookie jar!

She said we could go back to the house, that they would be there shortly. I felt so bad for her. Six months after Mom found her sobriety, she lost it. She had a very hard time coming out of this bout with alcohol. I knew in my heart that she had started drinking again. I knew the same feelings she had at starting. After all I knew her disease. I knew how many times one would swear she wouldn't do this again. The disappointment she must have felt in herself.

She did not need me ranting on her about her failing. I accepted it and accepted her. I prayed for her to a God I was getting to know, to help her find her sobriety again. To really be at peace with herself and truly be a happy person. She needed to forgive herself.

Chapter 22

JOB 3:4

Let that day be forever forgotten.

IN EARLY 1988, MOM WAS SPIRALING DOWN THIS BLACK TUNNEL of alcoholism. I would go to visit and there was never not a drink in front of her. I would look at her and see the puffiness in her face. She went to sleep drunk and arose with a glass in her hand. I knew that Mom was going to die if she kept this up. She could not even begin to quit on her own. Physically her body would never be able to stand the withdrawals from being away from the alcohol. I was now having my third child. My oldest brother Calvin (Cal, we called him), will enter into my life at this time. He was thirty-five years old. Much older than I at twenty-seven years old. He was always a hardworking man. And boy, did he like to tease! He had broken up with his second wife. He was depressed, but that comes with a marriage breakup. Reneta his wife, treated him like crap anyway, but you couldn't make him see that.

I was just a month from being due with my baby. He stopped over around six thirty in the evening. He had had a few beers, sitting at my table. He had just found out that my sister Connie's boyfriend was dying from brain cancer. He did not know how to cope with that. He told me it was unfair. He said he wished he had a wife who treated him well. He told me he was going out of town the next day to look for a job. He was having a hard time finding work

95

here, he said. He was renting an apartment. He said that he was going to be leaving most of his things at the apartment so he wanted me to move all his things to my garage to keep for him because he did not feel he would be back till after the rent was due.

So he left that night. I went up to his apartment a few days later and opened the door and it seemed like such a sad place. There was no light shining through the window. The curtains were closed. I thought that he must have felt so lonely there by himself. I tracked down those stairs with my brother's belongings. Thinking you're going to owe me big time, Cal! When you get home! Moving you! When I am so big and pregnant! Oh, yeah, you owe me big time! A couple days later. Peggy, my sister came by and asked if I had seen Cal.

I said, "Yes, he was over the other night and asked me to take care of his things, till he got back." He was going out of town to look for work. She asked me how he sounded? I said, "He was upset about Denny, Connie's boyfriend." But that he had joked on and off while he was there. The only thing I found kind of funny was that he had a real expensive stereo system. He was always telling the kids to leave it alone or they would break it. He asked me to take care of it for him. I just thought perhaps he did not have anywhere else to keep it. So I did not think any more about it.

Peggy thought something did not sound right with how he was acting. So once again we were going to the police station to report a loved one as missing. We reported that he just went through a second divorce. He was taking a friend's illness rather hard. Two weeks later, July 3, there was a knock at my door. It was one of the deputies on Cal's case. I opened the door and thought, *oh, he must have news about Cal.* He asked me if he could talk to me. I said, "Sure come in." He probably needs more information about him. He asked me to sit down and he told me they had found Cal's truck deep in the wooded area of an old abandoned, unused gravel pit by Garfield. I knew the place. Eleven years before we went and searched for Sandi there.

I asked if he was alive? He said, "I am sorry. He was found by a man cutting wood. The truck was buried under so much brush that he intended to stay hid forever." I asked how? He said, "Cal drilled a hole under the cab of his truck and ran a hose from the muffler up into this hole and put rags around it. He had asphyxiated himself. The shock at what he was telling me, I could not believe. Why? After all we had gone through with our sister! Why would you just end your life? How could he do this to us! To our mom! So we wanted everyone in our family notified before they announced it on TV. I went to Donnelly where Connie was working and thought on my ride I never had to tell anyone much less my sister that our brother was gone.

I would try to hold back by tears and try to find a less shocking way to tell her. But there was none. I walked up to the machine she was working on. She turned and smiled and said, "Oh, what are you doing here?" I tried not to cry. I told her they found Cal and that he was not alive. I started to turn away and I started to cry. Someone had to tell mom that Cal had passed away. Connie said she would go tell Mom.

The fourteenth of July, ten days after Cal was found, I had my son, Dallas. I remember being in labor and one minute being so happy and the next so heartbroken. On the seventeenth we buried our brother, Cal. I thought he would be alive if I would have just paid attention to his silent cries. The times he would come to see me and tell me he was depressed and me just think, he is, he would be, he is fighting to see his kids, he is getting a divorce from his second wife and she is pregnant. I thought, if I would have got my nose out of my life a little I would have probably been able to help him.

Instead he killed himself within hours of leaving my home that night. I asked myself, did he actually think no one cared for him? Did he feel so empty inside that he felt he was better off dead? I started to become angry with him, because he planned out with me in agreement. His last wishes. What he wanted done with his things. I thought how very unfair of him to use me like that and to deceive me! I, at that time, had very mixed emotions. One of great joy at the birth of my son. And one of great sorrow at the lonely sad suicide of my oldest brother.

I was released from the hospital the day of Cal's funeral. Denny, Connie's boyfriend, was there as an honorary pallbearer. He was too weak and sick to carry Cal's casket. I remember looking at him and *thinking, here is a man that wants to live so badly. Look at you, Cal, taking your own life for granted and just throwing it all away! Like your life didn't matter!* Then I watched his two boys as they looked upon their father's casket I wondered at all the pain he was causing. I was standing outside the church before the service and Mom and Kenny drove up. My real dad was standing beside Peggy, talking with her and watching from a distance as Mom got out of the truck and I could tell that she was drunk.

I felt such pity for her. This was the second child she had buried. I knew she wanted with all her heart to be sober. I watched her for a while and then I met her and hugged her, because she had come through so much. She loved her son the only way she knew how. My sister met her on the sidewalk, took her by the shoulders and asked her why she could not even come to her son's funeral sober and turned around and walked away. Leaving us alone, standing there. So I took Mom by the arm and I walked proudly beside her. Past the father, that never had anything to do with me. To let everyone know that no matter what, she was my mom! My father watched us walk by. It had been ten years since I had seen him and I thought, *yes, you watch, she never not once turned her back on me and pretended that I just never existed!* I walked with her and Kenny, as she went to say goodbye to her child, her firstborn son.

I left the church that day, feeling betrayed by Cal. He, I felt, used me as a pawn in his plan. I still find the urge to look down the road and see his truck coming and getting out and saying, "Oh, I would have gotten ahold of you all, but life's been great!" I pray to God that the man that found Cal, is so richly blessed. Not only for ending another search for us. But also for the memories he must carry of that day. We are back to our lives, just another sibling gone forever. Only to keep in our memories. Mom went back to living with the guilt of Cal's suicide and Sandi's murder, to her mother's abuse. I always felt I should have had the control to stop all these bad things from happening. I was the caretaker, even though I was not using anymore myself. I still felt like I should have been able to help Cal and not have to bury another family member.

Chapter 23

2 CORINTHIANS; 4:18

So we do not look at what we can see right now, the troubles all around us, but we look forward to the joys in heaven which we have not yet seen. The troubles will soon be over, but the joys to come will last forever.

IT WAS NOW 1988. ME AND MY HUSBAND LIVED UP AROUND VINING. We lived on a horse ranch. It was a beautiful place. Mom would come and visit, sometime even stay overnight. The house itself had been through its own tragedies. The previous owners had lost a boy to leukemia. And they had left everything and moved away. I had horses there and goats and chickens. Happy times! Acres and acres to ride. But the turmoil in my life was still there. My husband was never home. After being gone for a few days, he would come home sick, and ready to sleep. I had three kids now. One day he left to go drinking with his brother. I had my two nephews and one niece over to stay for the weekend and play with the kids. My husband had left early in the day. The kids spent the day playing outside. I had made homemade soup for supper and we had eaten.

In the evening, the kids wanted to have a sleep out down in the den. So I said sure. My youngest was a little over two, so he was sleeping in our bedroom instead of his room. My oldest son had fallen asleep on the couch in the living room. I had lain down beside my youngest when I heard the truck, so I got up. I knew it was the kids' dad. I was going to tell him he had to use the patio door because the kids had locked the den door. He got out of his brother's truck. I yelled down so he could hear me. He did not answer me. I went to get some soup ready for him. He came up the stairs. I was by the stove and I said, while looking down at the kettle, "I made some soup," and as I said that, I looked up. He was coming right for me!

I knew by the look on his face that he was not concerned with what I was saying; he only wanted to get me! I don't know how I knew it, but I did. I dropped the spoon and turned to run, thinking if I got into the bedroom that he would see his son laying there and he would leave me alone and come to his senses! I ran through the living room and into the bedroom. He was right behind me! That woke my oldest son up. But he pretended to stay asleep! I crawled in beside my sleeping baby and thought that he would not hurt our baby! He came in there and I said, "Be careful, I have the baby!" He jumped at me with no concern for him! I lay on my side trying to protect him. He kept pulling on my legs, trying to get me closer to him! He was trying to get ahold of my neck. He was hitting, not caring where his strikes landed!

I got myself higher in the bed and he was kind of crawling on the bed, coming towards me and I took both feet and kicked him! He went backwards and I took my son in those few minutes and ran, with my baby in my arms, through the living room. My son jumped up and followed close behind me! We ran downstairs to a bedroom that had a lock on it! I kept telling my baby not to cry! "Shh! Please be quiet. He's gonna find us! God, please, don't let him come down here!" The rest of the kids were in the den. I did not believe he would hurt them. I thought he was after me, not them.

I could hear him upstairs, walking back and forth, yelling, "I'm going to find you! You f—–en bitch! I'm gonna kill you!" Down the stairs he would come, yelling, "Where the f—– are you? I'm gonna kill you when I find you!" He went into the den and took the gun down off the gun rack. And said he was going to kill the kids, they got up and ran to the door going outside and he grabbed my oldest daughter's arm and she pulled away from him. They all ran outside and into the woods! Me and the boys did not know that he had gone after them.

He would walk almost to where we were hiding and I would say, "Please don't come to this room!" It was as though he would stop and turn around and go the other way. He finally went back upstairs. I could hear him in the kitchen, yelling, he was going to kill me and where was I! I would drift off to sleep, my eyes snapping open every time he hit the table with his fist! Around five in the morning, I got up. It was quiet. I told my son that maybe he fell asleep.

I opened the door and we peeked out, nothing! We went out into the hall and went in my daughter's room. The gun lay across her dresser! We went into the den and no kids! Where could they be? We went slowly up the stairs, the kitchen was empty. We went to the living room, no one, and into our bedroom. Everyone was gone! I went back into the kitchen to call my sister-in-law and I was standing there and the kids were peeking through the patio doors. They saw me standing there and came in. All talking at once! I stopped them and asked my daughter where her dad was?

She said, "A car came late in the night and he left with whoever it was." I asked them where they had been? They said they had spent the night in the woods! He had come after them and said he was going to kill them! They ran out and stayed in the woods, scared! I called his sister and told her what happened and that I did not know where he went! She said she picked him up, that he had called and said I had taken the kids and left. I told her that he was lying! He had gone crazy! She brought him back. He said I had brainwashed the kids into saying all that and I had made it all up.

The insanity of it all! He never once admitted to the terror he caused all of us that night. Forty-five years later, they all still talk about the night he went after them with a gun! The only thing he ever asked me to do was not tell the kids' parents. So I guess in the end, where the truth counted, he did know what he had done! My husband's brother Cory would come to the ranch to help cut wood. He stayed a couple of days. He was always such a sweet guy. He was nine years old when I met him for the first time. He would always want to stay at my house. Before I met his brother in the summer of 1989, Cory would have been twenty years old. He was at a party in Alexandria. Him and his friend were sitting on a bench by a tree outside and a guy walked up to him and shot Cory in the chest and ran. Cory did not at first know he got shot. He asked his friend next to him, "Who got shot?" He looked down at his chest, saw the blood and tumbled over. The ambulance came, he died on the operating table.

They caught the guy that shot Cory. He, I guess, was supposedly been angry with Cory. He went to trial. Pled guilty to murder in the second degree.

Received a twenty-year sentence. His name was Burger, he was released from prison in 2008. After serving a thirteen-year sentence. I watched at Cory's funeral, so much like my sister Sandi's death. A mother who cannot be consoled at the loss of her child. How I felt the system was lenient on these murderers. How another young life was snuffed out. To never be able to see the potential they could have been. Cory was buried at the Carlos Cemetery. Just one more tragedy to make its mark in my heart.

Chapter 24

PSALMS; 3: 6

And now, although ten thousand enemies surround me on every side, I am not afraid.

MOM DRANK STEADY FOR THE NEXT TWO YEARS. ONE DAY I WAS over there. She did not look well at all. She was bloated. I swore I would never send the police out there again to haul her away to detox! I needed to do something, though. She was killing herself! There was a man, who thirteen years earlier had become an angel to me. I went to his daughter, who was a counselor and asked her if her dad would go out and talk with Mom? Mom held such respect for him. I thought maybe she might listen to him and if she did not, nothing would change. But it was worth a try! He readily agreed to go out there and try to talk with her. I have no idea what George McKay ever said to Mom. I never questioned either him nor my mom about what was said. But the next day I went over to Mom's just to see if she would say anything about him. She said that George McKay had been out to see her.

I noticed she was not drinking. Then there were more days that she went without drinking. I do not nor will I ever know what he said to my mom that day. But he gave us a very special gift that day! A mom that was sober. One I had never had most of my entire life. He is the star in the heavens that shines next to my Saviors. My angel that came to help our family, in losing Sandi and saving our mom in a way I am sure he never imagined. Each new day brought greater strength to Mom. She started calling me and asking me to go to different places with her. She wanted to visit my sisters and brothers. She started coming over for coffee and she would spend the whole day. She would come spend the weekend.

She cut Kenny off the hard whiskey, and only let him have a couple of beers during the day. She bought herself a horse and a donkey. She loved animals! She had three little dogs; she called them her kids. She got a canary and I gave her two parakeets. She loved them. She used to feed the birds outside in the winter. The kids learned that Grandma was better. That there is always good inside the bad. She had them stay overnight with her. They would watch her sew. And she would make them things to wear! They grew to love her so much. I had lived for this day! God had finally answered my prayers. We had our real mom, the one I knew was under all that sickness. I would talk to Mom about her past. As much as she wanted to. Her mother abused her. I believe that contributed to her history of alcoholism. Also the tragic deaths of her two children just compounded her abuse. And a lot of guilt.

Mom was not good at communication with anyone about feelings. She had no one to confide in when she was young. "I love you" was never told to her when she was young. So she raised her children the same way she was raised. No, I never recall Mom telling me she loved me. But I knew in my heart she did! Just by her actions. In the following years, my mom became my life, my best friend. If we are ever to have a parent as a friend, she was mine, not to replace Sandi but to fill my life. I never worried that one day I would go to her house and she would be drinking. It was as if Jesus had bestowed such a powerful healing on my mom, that there was never any yearning for her to take another drink again! I talked with her about our drinking. I told her that although it had been a couple years since I drank, there were still times where I wanted to go and just have a couple.

I would say, "Mom, you ever feel like that?"

She always would tell me, "No, I don't have the want of it." So, Jesus gave Mom the healing from deep within. Where everything that happened was washed away and she was made clean! The deaths of her children were only a blessed assurance that she would be reunited with them in heaven. To be truly happy, as she never could be here on earth.

Mom became a more patient person. She was more at ease with herself. Things that use to bother her and irritate her, really did not affect her like they had before. She seemed at peace with herself. She did not seem to feel that every bad thing that happened was because of something she had done and was her fault. In 1990, I was going to have my fourth child. Mom had been sober for three years! I was thirty years old. Loving my mom! She and Kenny would come every weekend and spend the day. If she didn't come over, I was calling her. Always asking her for the same recipe. I think she liked that if I was not calling her, she was calling me! Or I would be at her place.

We went to sales every weekend. I think Mom thrived on miscellaneous auction sales! She loved them! But so did I. That is how we spent our weekends, always finding an auction sale to go to. Rain or shine! She would buy something for me that she thought I would like. I would buy something for her that I thought she would like. And that is how we told each other we loved each other. We seemed to never need the words we knew. I decided that if I would ever get to have a sober mom, I would spend every day with her if I could. I honored my mom. I would never ever say anything that would make her unhappy. I had the real her now, not the chemical-induced mom that I could never carry on a conversation with, but still loved her more than myself. Did I ever regret the time I spent with my mom? "No!" But it did cause a lot of hard feelings between my husband and myself. To this day I still do not regret the time I had with her. And cherish the time she spent with me.

On August 28, mom came over and went to the doctor with me. I was two-weeks overdue and I felt just miserable! The doctor told me, "Well, it should be any time now, head's down, it just has to decide when it's coming!" An hour later we were coming back home and I went into labor.

I told my husband that I thought it was time to go, and Mom smiled and said. "That baby isn't going to be born till after six o'clock tonight!" We left and went to the hospital and my little girl was born twenty minutes later! The doctor didn't even get his scrubs on! I called Mom at my house and she said, "Boy, that was fast! On August 31, I was taken into surgery and came out to never have children again. That was not my choice, more so my husband's and his mom's. Being the people pleaser that I was. I didn't want anyone mad or disappointed in me. Stuffing my feelings and what I wanted back down my throat, even if I choked on it. I was such a bad person anyway, that this was just another form of punishment that I felt I deserved.

Mom was always there for me. When I came home from the hospital with my daughter, I could never tell my mom that now I was different. Would have the scar to remind me for the rest of my life. I was nothing now! I was empty, something that was so important to me was gone forever! I just could not explain, no one would understand how I felt! I never wanted to do this! It seemed like a part of me was lost, gone forever. I lost myself somewhere, I turned my back on my values. I blamed my husband and his mother for making these choices for me. I shut those doors and locked them tight! There was so much hurt there., I never wanted to look at that empty pain again!

My only surviving brother, Lonnie.

Chapter 25

JOHN; 12:44–50

"If you trust me, you are really trusting God. For when you see me, you are seeing the one who sent me. I have come as a Light to shine in this dark world, so that all who put their trust in me will no longer wander in the darkness. If anyone hears me and doesn't obey me. I am not his judge, for I have come to save this world and not to judge it. But all who reject me and my message will be judged at the Day of Judgment by the truths I have spoken. For these are not my own ideas, but I have told you what the Father said to tell you. And I know his instructions lead to eternal life, so whatever he tells me to say, I say!"

IN NOVEMBER OF '92, MY MOM'S SISTER VIRGINIA PASSED AWAY. It was a hard day for my mom. If Mom was close to any of her siblings, it had to be Ginny. I, on the other hand, only remember the lady who met me at the milk house door. I really did not feel a loss at my aunt's passing. I really felt nothing at all. About a week after her death, my uncle called me. He asked if I could come down to his place to visit. I was now thirty-three years old. I thought he was lonely. So I said sure, I would be down there on the following Sunday. I called and told my mom that he wanted to see me. She said she thought that was a good idea.

So I arrived and I made the small talk, asked how he was, if he was doing okay since Ginny's death. He told me that he needed to tell me something. So

I sat there that day and listened to him tell the story of long years ago. Before I was ever born. How Aunt Ginny could never have kids. So they—being Mom and Dad—swapped partners in the hopes that Ginny would become pregnant by my father. But instead Mom became pregnant with me. My uncle was actually my father!

He made it sound so flippant, like it was no big deal! "Past is the past," he said. "You're okay with all this, right?" I told him of course, yes, no big deal. But my heart was screaming, *"Why did you all have to do this to me?"* Now I knew why my dad hated the sight of me! Because he knew I did not belong to him! Now I knew why, for two years, I was punished by my aunt! Every time she looked at me, she was reminded of the pact they had all made! She ended up regretting it, so I was the one who took the punishment for their actions! I wanted to yell at him, ask him who he thought he was! The hell I went through! No one ever wanted me except my mom! I wanted to tell him exactly what his wife put me through all those years ago! He never in thirty-two years claimed me as his daughter, until his wife passed away. I wanted to say many things to him that day! But instead, I smiled and said I understood. I went away from there, thinking the only one who wanted to claim me as theirs was my mom. I was thirty-two years old. I did not need a father now!

I would go visit him and he would come visit me. It all felt so fake. Slowly through time I visited less. His niece was very jealous of me. Thought I was after his money. He would take me out to lunch and introduce me to his friends as his daughter. I would feel embarrassed and like it was not real. We were both pretending feelings we never had for each other. I belonged to no one except my mom. Am I one hundred percent sure he is my real father? No! And really it didn't matter. All my life I had only one parent and I was okay with that now.

In '93 Mom had been sober for six years! She was having some blood pressure issues and started to see a doctor in Osakis where Peggy doctored. I took her down there a couple times. They put her on a high blood pressure medication and she said it made her sick. So she asked me if I could make her an appointment with my doctor in Henning, Minnesota. She said that she had to have her medication changed and that his office visits were cheaper than the doctor in Osakis.

So I made the appointment. I took her in to see him. He said that the doctor in Osakis had her on too much medication. That was why it was making her sick. He prescribed a lesser dose and told her if everything was going well, he would see her in three months. She seemed to like him. He paid attention to what she was saying, she had said. At this point she came to my house once in a while. Otherwise, she was spending more time with my two brothers. They had a little farm that my mom just fell in love with. She went out there and put lawn ornaments out in the yard, she planted a whole bunch of flowers, and helped plant a garden there. She had an old Volkswagen camper and she moved it out there and had made curtains for the windows and she was going to spend her time there once in a while. She said the place was so peaceful and quiet there. I swear she really loved that place. It became her second home away from home!

Mom came to spend the night. Early in the day, I cut her hair and gave her a perm. She had such baby-fine hair. She kept telling me to make sure the rollers were tight! I told her I didn't want to hurt her or pull her hair. I said to her, that her hair was like combing baby hair! I cut her hair short. I think she liked it because she kept going to the mirror and primping. I told her we would wait a week, and then we would dye her hair. So we went to bed and the next day she went home and said she and Kenny would be back on the weekend to go to the auction sale. I was now thirty-three years old. I was happy basically. I had my mom and I cherished every day I spent with my sober mom! I knew her as a whole new person, the one I always knew was buried deep inside.

Mom and Kenny came on Saturday. It was so hot that July day! It was the twenty-sixth of July. We left and went to the auction sale. We sat on the bleachers for a while and Mom moved and went down to sit in a booth. I watched her for a while, and then I went down and sat by her. I asked her if she was feeling okay. She said she had a bit of a headache, said it was because of the heat. We stayed for the rest of the sale. Later we got ready to go. She and Kenny got in their truck and she said she would see me Tuesday, so I could dye her hair. I told her I would call her later.

Monday, July 27, in the afternoon I was getting supper ready and I felt so sad. I could have just sat and cried. I thought I was just tired. I set the table and said it was time to eat. My husband asked if I was going to eat and I told him no, I didn't feel like eating. A few minutes later the phone rang, my daughter answered it. She said it was for me, I took the phone, and it was Kenny; he was crying. All he said was they had taken Mom to the hospital by ambulance!

109

I could not believe what I had heard. I hung up the phone and my whole body was shaking! I said, "They took Mom to the hospital. I am leaving!"

On the way there, I prayed every prayer I knew! I begged her to wait! That I would take care of her and make everything better! But she had to wait till I got there! I was driving eighty- five miles an hour! I came to the last stop sign before Alexandria and I just stopped and cried. "No! You just have to wait for me, Mom! Everything will be okay!" I walked into the hospital and went to the front desk. I asked them if they brought in Zelda Haabala? They asked me when she was born? I told them March 31, 1934. They would not tell me where she was!

I asked them if she was okay? They told me that some of the family was in a private waiting room. I asked them again if she was okay! All they said was that some of the family was in this waiting room and I could go there and wait. So a nurse came and took me to this room. The door was opened and there sat Kathy and Peggy. I stood in the doorway and I looked at Peggy and all she said was she was dead.

"No!" I cried. "No, No, No!" It was as if someone had pulled my whole heart out! I sank down to my knees in that waiting room. I cried as so many years ago Mom had cried for the loss of the children she gave birth to. I was crying for the one who gave me the very life I had. I repeated in that room to her somewhere, that she was supposed to wait for me, that I would have made it okay! Why did you not wait for me? They were going to sedate me, but I refused. They asked us if we wanted to see her before they transported her to the funeral home. We said yes, and me and Kathy and her husband went in first. The door was closed. Part of me wanted to run so very far away, to not have to face this! But the other part needed my mom so very much. The door was opened slowly and every inch of my body was shaking. I stepped to the edge of the bed, she looked as though she were asleep.

I touched her hands and they were still so very warm and soft. I finally said what I could never say out loud to her. That I loved her and that she was the best mom ever; no matter what had happened, my love had never changed through anything! I bent and kissed her softly on the cheek. As I left I wondered how I would ever be able to go on without her. I had to go to the little farm that she had loved so much and tell my brothers that our mom was gone. I drove back to Parkers Prairie in a fog. Went to the little farm, the boys were there. I thought to myself, *How many times have we done this, driven to tell a family member someone else was gone from our family?*

Oscar came outside when I drove up. He smiled and asked what I was up to? I asked him where Lonnie was. He said he was in the house, in the bathroom.

Lonnie came out and asked, "What you doing, out bummin?"

I said, "Mom was taken to the hospital and she passed away."

Lonnie went back in the bathroom and Oscar went outside. I left there and went back home and went to the den and sat in the dark and I cried and I died. I changed completely. I had bitterness and anger and hate and betrayal inside my heart. I wanted no one around me. I was lost and could not find my way out of this sadness. This was different than Sandi and Cal's deaths. This was my mom! How did I begin to get over this. Of never having someone there to call my mom! So I left myself in this dark place, to be alone with my loss, a wound that I could never begin to know how to heal. People could not understand that my life had stopped, that I could not keep going. She was such an everyday part of my life. That to have a day without her in it, was not life to me; it was death to me! I did not want to wake up and not have her here. I did not want to go pick out a casket for her. I did not want to go get her an outfit to wear, just to have to bury her in it! I wanted to see her alive!

We went to the funeral home to decide on a casket for our mom. I left the office in tears. We went to the lawyer's office. I just could not do this! We did all the things you're supposed to do in this kind of situation. We laid Mom to rest beside Sandi, where she always said she wanted to be. Mom looked so beautiful, in death. So at peace. The etches of life's pain gone from her face. No more heartaches, no more sadness. I knew in my heart right then, that Mom was where her soul longed to be, with her children in heaven. The peace that held her face was to show us she was happy now, truly happy! I have God and Chief George McKay to thank for giving her the chance to walk the path that led her back to her children. I have no regrets for who she was way back then, many years ago. It was who she became! What a great woman! Mom's favorite hymn was, "Amazing Grace"—how sweet the sound that saved a wretch like me! I once was lost. But now am found, was blind, but now I see!

Chapter 26

PSALMS 24:5

They will receive God's own goodness as their blessings from him, planted in their lives by God himself, their Savior.

I BELIEVE WHAT STARTED OUT AS SANDI'S STORY, WAS IN FACT my story! How I felt about my sister's death and how I tried to cope with all the alcoholism that I was living with and later becoming an alcoholic myself, and marrying into it. I must say I have grown, not so much in understanding how people can be so cruel to one another and show such little regard for human life, no! I will probably never grow to understand that part of human nature. But I have come to understand that no matter what, the seed of sickness, be it alcoholism, drugs, or even violence, Such as Sandi's family went through, you have the need to forgive the accused in order to recover. You cannot carry the seed of hatred for what was done to you. You can never keep the hurt inside you and pretend it never happened. That creates a greater sickness than the actual sickness itself. And you will always remain their victim. The ability to forgive someone of the hardest thing possible. Taking someone you love away in a violent act is a very hard thing to forgive. Sandi was more than a sister; she was my best friend. We helped each other survive the foster homes, the drinking, the fighting. We always stuck together, like an extra arm or leg. I felt a great hatred toward the man. I think its natural. It is part of the grieving process that we go through, and then we must heal and learn from the experience also.

Just as when little and you stuck you tongue on that old pump handle outside in the winter and it stuck there fast and instead of getting your tongue wet first, we just yanked it off and left the skin there. Enough to let you know you would never do that again. So we learn! Such a painful experience but, you learn that the world, no matter if you're in the city of ten thousand or a town of three hundred. Violence can and will occur anywhere.

I will never say that my life after these events became beautiful. I had another murder in my life in 2004. My brother in 2012 was diagnosed with leukemia, and I took a nine-month journey with him and my sister. That's another book in itself. A search for a sister who vanished for twelve days and all the memories it brought back of my sister Sandi's abduction and murder. I do know everything belongs to God. Each day we rise and thank him for our eyes that have opened. We lay down and we thank him for the day and all those who shared this day. I now never question the whys. They are not for me to know, just try to learn from them. The people who went to be with our Savior, were the most important part of my life. I never took their deaths well; it shattered me to the core. But today I visit their graves and I feel a peace; one day they will be coming to meet me and the whys won't matter.

I miss them all terribly and it still brings tears to my eyes when I think about them. Today it's not so much about the sadness of not having them here. It's about the deep love I had for each one of them. And the different kinds of love I had for them. God loves me, this I am for sure! He has blessed me abundantly with these special people I had the chance to share my growing-up years with. Those who taught me how to overcome the greatest obstacles. One day Jesus will open up his arms to receive me in his and none of this world will matter. I praise Jesus for the day he gave me my mom, Calvin, my sister Sandi and my brother Oscar and my grandbaby Avryonna or, for that matter, all my family.

*These are my remaining sisters left to right
Jean, Peggy, Connie and Kathy*

*Our brother Calvin, right our dad Calvin, Our dearest Sandi, bottom,
our brother Oscar, My granddaughter Avryonna, My sweet, sweet mom
and my best stepfather Ray Haabala. We love you all.*